THE COMMER
   OF THE I
      95

The Commercial Revolution of the Middle Ages
950-1350

ROBERT S. LOPEZ

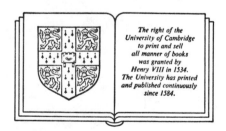

The right of the
University of Cambridge
to print and sell
all manner of books
was granted by
Henry VIII in 1534.
The University has printed
and published continuously
since 1584.

CAMBRIDGE UNIVERSITY PRESS

Cambridge

London   New York   New Rochelle

Melbourne   Sydney

Published by the Press Syndicate of the University of Cambridge
The Pitt Building, Trumpington Street, Cambridge CB2 1RP
32 East 57th Street, New York, NY 10022, USA
10 Stamford Road, Oakleigh, Melbourne 3166, Australia

© Cambridge University Press 1976

First published 1971 by Prentice-Hall, Inc.
First published by Cambridge University Press 1976
Reprinted 1977, 1979, 1982, 1984, 1985, 1986

Printed in the United States of America

ISBN 0 521 21111 5 hard covers
ISBN 0 521 29046 5 paperback

To
The Yale Department of History,
with admiration and gratitude

Preface

This little book aims at showing a rather unfamiliar facet of medieval Europe's image: not cathedrals and castles, but, mainly, the walled cities and open country that were the stage of a commercial revolution between the tenth and the fourteenth centuries. Here, for the first time in history, an underdeveloped society succeeded in developing itself, mostly by its own efforts.

Such a statement could of course be challenged. It may be argued that men have been developing ever since they diverged from monkeys, or that the New Stone Age marked a steep acceleration as compared to the Old Stone Age, or that the ancient civilizations of Egypt, Mesopotamia, and China increased their production beyond comparison with their prehistoric predecessors. On the other hand, it may be observed that growth during the Commercial Revolution of the European Middle Ages was far slower than during the Industrial Revolution of the modern period, which in turn fell short of the breath-taking tempo of our own time.

All this is true, but economic development in each of its premedieval phases came to a full stop before the ceiling of what we would today call an underdeveloped society was broken. And if medieval growth was not fast, it was altogether irreversible; it created the indispensable material and moral conditions for a thousand years of virtually uninterrupted growth; and, in more than one way, it is still with us. Today, as we endeavor to keep growing amid prophecies of impending doom, and as we try to promote growth in underdeveloped countries, we have something to learn by studying the circumstances of the medieval take-off.

One cannot summarize four centuries of European economic history in less than two hundred pages without constant oversimplification. This is especially dangerous when documents are inadequate, quantitative data unavailable, and interpretations controversial. In order to pay sufficient attention to the leading role of commerce, which seems to me the great turning point of medieval economy, I may have understressed agriculture because it was less dynamic, religious and political theories because they were less influential, institutional and cultural by-products because they were less central to the process. The reader, I hope, will look for what I have said and not for what I have regretfully omitted. By appending a very sketchy bibliographic note I offer him some ammunition to shoot at my possible and probable distortions and errors. That they are not more numerous I owe in part to a grant from the National Foundation for the Humanities, which has enabled me to fill many gaps in my knowledge of urban development.

Even the shortest historical essay must carry acknowledgments. Let them be brief. Once more, as in my earlier books, they begin at home: my wife, my mother, my children, my family in Milan and Brussels have done much more than reading parts of the manuscript: they have given healthy aeration to my ivory tower. Etienne Kirschen, my brother-in-law, has plugged a few cracks in my analysis of economic growth, for in my approach to economic history I see "economic" as an important attribute, but the noun is "history." Teachers, colleagues and students to whom I feel indebted are too many for individual mention; I may single out Harry Miskimin, who has played in turn the roles of student, colleague, and adviser, and embrace all others in a collective expression of thanks. Finally, I shall pay tribute to the dead, who are the staunch friends of every historian: medieval dead such as Francesco di Balduccio Pegolotti, an authority on commerce, or Walter of Henley, an authority on farming; and recent, beloved dead such as Gino Luzzatto, who cautioned me against stretching sources beyond what they really say, and my father, Sabatino Lopez, who planted in me the impression that there may be some good in man, even though evil yields higher economic returns.

Contents

ix

1

Roman and Barbarian Precedents

THE GRANDEUR THAT
WAS ROME

History is an ever-changing continuum; without some account of the earlier period, we can hardly understand why the Commercial Revolution was at the same time the end product of a long tradition and the beginning of a new one.

The great expansion of the later Middle Ages succeeded a great contraction in the early Middle Ages, which in turn had come after the expansion of the Classic Ages. This alternation of crest, trough, and crest can be observed not only in the economic field, but in almost every aspect of life: literature and art, philosophy and thought, politics and law also were affected, though not all to the same extent. The greatest achievements of the Greeks and the Romans were not in the economic field; yet the inventiveness of the former and the efficiency of the latter were more than enough to make the Greco-Roman economy the most successful one in the recorded history of antiquity. Let us take a quick glance at its main traits in the prime of the Roman Empire, that is, approximately, from Augustus (29 B.C.–A.D. 14) to Marcus Aurelius (161–180).

All along the broad belt of territory around the Mediterranean Sea, which formed the spine of the Empire, the population had grown and lengthened its life expectancy. It is true that the average span was about twenty-five years, but this is not much less than that of Egypt in 1948 (thirty-one years) or China in 1946 (thirty-five years), which had then both been affected by another fifteen centuries of medical and technological progress. The elites in the Roman towns and the large country estates lived in luxury. A substantial middle class enjoyed a comfortable existence. Town laborers and peasants were much worse off, but there is virtually no archaeological evidence that they were afflicted by such malnutrition diseases as India, for instance, has not yet been able to stamp out. Slavery was a tragic scourge, but the number of slaves was diminishing; their condition had generally improved; and there may have been some truth to the statement of a Roman ambassador at the court of Attila the Hun: "We, the Romans, treat our slaves better than you treat your free subjects." At any rate, a freed slave became every inch a man, and his son could aspire to the highest positions. Though class consciousness was always present, the Romans had no use for racism. Naturally they felt superior to the untamed and unpolished nations beyond their frontiers, but they were willing to teach their civilization and way of life to the "barbarians" who individually or in group, spontaneously or under pressure, came under their rule. Thus the greatest melting pot in history went to work: many nations became one, and eventually all free men within the Empire shared the burdens and the benefits of citizenship.

The formation of such a large community, which enjoyed for more than two centuries (the first and second after Christ) the blessings of low taxation, security, and almost unbroken internal peace, was bound to open extraordinary economic opportunities. The Roman Empire constituted a home market stretching from England to Egypt and from Morocco to Armenia, knit together by the Mediterranean and the military roads leading to the interior, and welded by a basic uniformity of tastes, living standards and class distribution. The imposing ruins of Roman theaters, bathhouses, and other community buildings, mostly erected by private contributions but open to all, still bear witness to the economic power of the richer citizens. The abundant and often refined equipment retrieved from the ashes of Pompei, the sands of Leptis Magna, or the mud of London reflects the high level of production for the commoners in every provincial town. Essential foodstuffs were easily available: the accumulated fragments of earthen containers for imported olive oil, dumped outside the urban wall, added an eighth hill (Mount Testaccio) to the original seven of Rome. The Romans planted vineyards wherever the climate consented; more important, they made drinkable water available everywhere. No doubt they were less imaginative and searching than the Greeks, but they knew better the value of material conveniences. As Frontinus, one of the directors of the imperial water service, put it, "Who would compare with our mighty aqueducts the idle Pyramids or the famous but useless works of the Greeks?"

Still, in their justified impression that they were well off, the Romans let go the greatest of all opportunities: economic growth. Growth, of course, is upsetting and tends to lose its appeal once a satisfactory equilibrium has been attained. This holds in economics as well as in art, in politics, and in war. Each of the great empires which had flourished before Rome sooner or later had grown up to such a point that it found a comfortable level, and sought no further. Similarly, in the last two centuries before Christ, republican Rome had matched her breathless military expansion with a measure of entrepreneurship and commercial adventure; but the political convulsions which accompanied that growth scared the landed aristocrats who originally held the power, and who eventually won the day. Augustus restored peace and dedicated the Empire to agricultural tranquillity and the pursuit of the golden mean, "aurea mediocritas." Every citizen was made to feel safe and well-adjusted to the standard of living to which his social position entitled him, but he was not encouraged to strive for more. Stability, not opportunity, was held out as the most desirable goal.

ROMAN AGRICULTURE

The conservative ideal of the Roman empire found its mainstay in agriculture, which was the occupation of the overwhelming majority, and the most respected source of revenue for the rich and the poor alike. By the time of Augustus, classic husbandry had achieved its highest degree of sophistication, and the basic formulae for the exploitation of the soil had hardened.

In general, the Romans employed manpower unsparingly to get

from the minimum of land the largest amount of vegetable calories. The virtues and the limitations of their methods were rooted in the ground and conditioned by the climate of Greece and peninsular Italy, the original homes of classic culture. Both countries are sheltered from excessive changes of temperature and well endowed with sunshine; the usually thin and light layer of cultivable earth answers readily to the farmer's care, and it is possible for the population to live healthily on a diet of cereals, roots, olives, fruits, and wine, without much meat. On the other hand, water resources are scant and unevenly distributed during the year; there are but few stretches of flat ground, many rocks and stones, and the long dry spells tend to reduce to dust the vegetable mould. Sudden, heavy rainfalls may then carry the dust downhill, ultimately obstructing the flow of rivers into the sea and forming mosquito-ridden marshes. Forests on mountain tops and slopes offer a natural defense against erosion; but they are seldom thick, and they yield too easily to the axe of the lumberman, the plough of the farmer, and eventually the teeth of goats and sheep which take turns in baring the wooded areas and keeping them bare.

Had the Greek and Roman farmers been unaware of these dangers, they would soon have reduced their countries to deserts. They did, however, display remarkable skill and perseverance in soil conservation. Only the best land was cropped every year (in some cases as much as three times a year), but with a suitable alternation of crops. On inferior soil, it was normal to let the land rest every second year. Animal manure, ashes and marls, alfalfa and other fertilizing plants were widely used. On steep declivities, the farmers offset the pull of gravity by organizing the earth into a series of terraces; they built reservoirs and canals to preserve and distribute the precious water. Above all—and this is the essence of what we still call "dry farming"—they spread moisture deep below the sun-parched surface by repeated criss-cross plowing, light plowing, of course, or else the mould would be ground into powder. A large proportion of the agricultural operations were done by hand, with small, ingenious tools; as regards livestock, the farmers preferred small animals, easily fed on what could not be used by men. Thus the good land was cultivated almost like a garden; it produced enough to support a dense population of frugal eaters, but the individual food producers had little surplus after they had fed themselves with whatever they could raise on their small rectangles of land.

In the long run, however, the very success of classic agriculture tended to upset the tight balance between manpower and crops. Peasant families, assured of comfortable subsistence and full employment, would grow and multiply until they saturated the country; then they had to encroach upon pastures, woods, and even the portion of land that was saved for the alternation of cropping and fallow. The dearth of pastures further restricted the number of horses and oxen that might save human labor in transportation and farming. Donkeys, goats, and sheep were inferior substitutes, which required no choice fodder but yielded hardly enough labor, meat, milk, and manure to make up for what they ate. Thus, in the long run, over-cropping and deforestation got the better of the ingenuity and hard work of the farmers, and the soil could no longer feed the large labor force without which dry farming could not be successful. Then the land had to be abandoned to sheep and goats, until further degradation transformed it into stony deserts on top and marshy wasteland at bottom.

Still, saturation was not inevitable so long as intensive agriculture could spill over into freshly conquered, sparsely settled barbarian territories. When peninsular Italy became too crowded, Roman farmers established colonies in the northern Italian plain and in the fertile belt of North Africa. Here, and in the other provinces which were successively annexed and colonized, better conditions of soil and climate made it possible to relax somewhat the requirements of Mediterranean dry farming. The traditional chessboard pattern of intensively cultivated fields was modified to allow more room for grazing grounds and woods, but there was no radical change from an economy of saturation to one of abundance, because farmers do not easily give up their customary ways and are slow in taking over whatever good there may be in the ways of less advanced neighbors. Moreover, the frontier ceased to advance as the Empire embraced peace, and settlements tightened up. Even so, down to the last centuries of imperial Rome the northern regions next to the border of Gaul and Germany remained comparatively prosperous, and northern Italy was not in serious distress, while wide stretches of peninsular Italy and Greece had become wildernesses contended between goats and wolves, and waiting for any barbarians who could step in and make some use of the land.

ROMAN COMMERCE AND INDUSTRY

Though most farmers and peasants individually produced very little surplus, the aggregated surplus of millions of agricultural workers was easily enough to support a large number of towns and to foster the development of industry, commerce, and banking. Much as they admired agriculture and depended on it, the Romans literally identified "civilization" with cities (*civitates*). Only a few of these were fairly large (Rome itself can hardly have contained much more than two hundred thousand inhabitants within the Aurelian walls of the late third century), and the five hundred "cities" of Roman North Africa may have averaged less than two thousand inhabitants each; their population was swollen by landed proprietors and farm laborers, and their prime *raison d'être* was political and administrative rather than economic. Still, there were artisans and shopkeepers in every town; there were landowners who drew considerable incomes by exploiting large estates through the work of undernourished slaves and depressed tenants; there were tax farmers,[1] manufacturers of military stores, contractors of public works, transport agents, loansharks, and many other traders who took advantage of the opportunities offered by the gigantic size of the Roman Empire. In turn, their concentrated purchasing power, added to that of millions of poorer consumers, formed a substantial total. For a long time, the Empire was at peace, taxes were moderate, and internal duties almost insignificant. There was no dearth of mineral resources, and the imperial mints relentlessly struck gold coins for the larger transactions, silver for the more ordinary ones, and copper for daily needs.

Under these circumstances, one may ask why the Roman economy remained so close to subsistence level, and why industry, commerce, and finance never really took off. Because ours is an industrial civi-

---

[1] Individuals who paid a fixed sum for the privilege of collecting taxes.

lization, contemporary economists tend to consider industrialization as the keystone of economic build-up; because credit plays a paramount role in financing new industries, they often look at it as the magic rod to stir up sleeping potentials of growth. History, however, seems to warn us that in an underdeveloped country credit does not come easily to those who lack capital, and commercialization has to precede industrialization. A merchant who will take risks and exploit price differences from one place to another may rapidly transform a small initial investment into a sizable capital. He may then use all or part of his gains to promote industrial development and market the products; he may also extend credit to other merchants, with an eye to business opportunities rather than to usurious returns from consumption loans to the poor and the spendthrift.

In the Roman Empire, however, the scope of commercial enterprise was restricted not only by the ordinary shortcomings of underdeveloped economies, but also by peculiar limitations in both of the fields where high rewards were possible: indispensable goods for the masses, luxuries for the choosy rich. The government took over in full or in part the production and distribution of salt, grain, metals, marble, and military uniforms. Foreign trade was severely handicapped by laws which, had they been rigidly enforced, would have forbidden the export of gold, strategic materials, foodstuffs, and almost anything that a foreigner might accept in exchange for his own goods. At any rate, not many foreign goods were desired in an Empire which produced almost everything it cared for. Interregional commerce within the Empire was more lively, but dwindled as the entire Roman world became more and more uniform. Differences in latitude, and hence in climate, are not exceedingly great between one Mediterranean region and another; wherever they went, the Romans planted the vegetables and trees which they liked, and shunned both the far North, where grapes would not ripen, and the far South, where olive trees would not grow. Likewise, provincial craftsmen gradually learned to imitate the best industrial products of Greece and Italy; the specialties of other regions were either adopted and copied everywhere or crowded out by more fashionable models.

The most serious obstacle to commercial development, however, was a psychological one. Trade was regarded as a base occupation, unworthy of gentlemen though not really unbecoming for commoners who would be unable to find a more dignified means of support. This prejudiced view was sanctioned by laws which, purportedly in order to make it easier for poorer people to earn their living, forbade noblemen to engage in commerce. It is true that long-distance commerce, when carried out on a large scale, was "not so very discreditable" (to use Cicero's judgment); still a man of that profession could fully redeem himself only if he retired from business as soon as he had gathered enough money to buy land and live like a gentleman. There were, of course, grasping men whom no legal or social disapproval could stop; we do hear of senators exercising petty trade through men of straw, and of plebeians trying to pass off as respectable men while clinging to their well-established export-import business. Nevertheless, the bad odor of commerce encouraged the natural propensity of affluent landowners to dissipate their capital in conspicuous consumption, and enticed status-seeking merchants to sink in uneventful agriculture the accumulated assets of thriving commercial enterprises. It also led the government to disregard trade in its planning.

One notable consequence was that the great military roads, built and kept up at staggering public expense, were too narrow for large carts and often had gradients too steep for any carts. Since pack animals were then extremely expensive, and transporting a standard cartload of hay over thirty miles doubled its price, long-distance commerce had to depend almost entirely on transportation by water. This, too, was taxed by the government's frequent requisitions of ships; but it was definitely cheaper. In fact, transportation by water ranked next to long-distance trade as a business where a daring entrepreneur could attain a fairly high economic reward.

CRAFTS AND CREDIT

With a few exceptions, craftsmen and industrial workers were at the bottom of the social ladder and had the smallest opportunities for economic self-improvement. Industries requiring strength rather than ability, such as mining, were almost entirely manned by slaves and convicts, and the competition of slaves contributed heavily to depress the earnings of even the most skilled free artisans. The Roman republic, when political strife was bitter and social mobility greater, had outlawed all craft guilds. The early Empire permitted them only on condition that they concern themselves solely with religious ceremonies and charitable purposes. The late Empire made them responsible for the regular delivery of a fixed quota of products, regardless of manpower supply and of market opportunities. No doubt passive resistance, strikes, and flight from work were not entirely unheard of, but at no time were guilds allowed to strive for collective action in defense of the craftsmen's own interests. And though there must have been a few success stories, it was extremely difficult for individual artisans to gain wealth and status through the work of their hands.

What kept industry down to a very low level of productivity was its inadequate mechanization, a much more serious shortcoming than inadequate animal power was for agriculture. Yet machines of various kinds had been invented and were used in ambitious projects, such as public buildings, hydraulic works, and highway construction. All this, however, required capital, and capital was in the hands of landowners who had no mind for industry (or, at most, drafted their slaves and tenants to make bricks, tools, and other agricultural implements for their own large estates); of merchants who could spare little beyond their investment in commerce proper; and of a government whose economic goals went no further than insuring stability, peace, and bread for all. It is said that when someone suggested to Emperor Vespasian to employ in public constructions a machine which would lift more weight than a whole team of workers, he replied, "Let me rather give food and work to these poor people." Without capital, and hence with modest tools, a craftsman soon reached the ceiling of the production he could achieve single-handedly. This in turn tended to create a closed circle: he produced little surplus because he lacked labor-saving devices and money to hire many assistants, and could not buy the devices or hire the assistants because he produced little surplus. No doubt the circle could be broken if he found somebody willing to lend him capital; but the low return of the investment made it impossible for him to obtain credit at reasonable terms.

Credit, at any rate, played a modest role in the Roman economy. Lending money at interest was not illegal, but was regarded as still more despicable than engaging in trade; for, as the philosophers taught, money is not consumed by the user and, unlike trees, does not bear fruit. It certainly bore no fruit in terms of economic growth when invested in consumption loans to the destitute and the spendthrift; such loans carried the highest charges and for that reason attracted the capital of greedy men of all classes. Money changers and deposit bankers lent to merchants at lower rates, but were hamstrung by the mediocrity of the business world, and never grew into something that could be remotely compared to modern commercial and industrial development banks. Credit was a will-o'-the-wisp when it was not usurious pawnbroking; the prudent, conservative spirit of the Roman society could hardly conceive wealth otherwise than as a tangible collection of fields, houses, cattle, slaves, movable objects, or hard cash. This view proved so compelling for the imperial government that when wars and other emergencies forced it to spend more than it received through ordinary taxation, it did not try to bridge the gap by borrowing from the citizens against the collateral of its immense assets. Extraordinary taxation and currency debasement were carried farther and farther, until all sources were exhausted and the Empire became disastrously insolvent without ever contracting any debts.

THE COLLAPSE OF THE EMPIRE
AND THE LONG DOWNWARD
TREND

It is hardly necessary to say that in recorded history, peace is a rare, almost abnormal phenomenon. The two relatively peaceful centuries of the early Empire were but a long interlude between the three centuries of offensive wars which built up the Roman commonwealth and the three centuries of defensive wars which brought it down. By 476, the western half of the Empire had been completely overrun by the "Barbarians" (that is, "foreigners," most of whom spoke Germanic languages). Yet the invaders were less numerous, less formidable, and, in general, more backward than the Greco-

Roman community; almost to the last minute, they accepted invitations to immigrate peacefully as mercenaries, allies, and future citizens; they conquered not by their own strength but by Roman default.

Why did the Roman will and ability to resist wear out? If we leave aside the possible impact of psychological changes, which cannot be adequately explored in the framework of economic history, the cause that immediately comes to mind is the relentless, increasing financial strain, amply documented as early as the late second century A.D. In the long run, the Empire could provide the money and manpower needed to hold back the Barbarians only by crushing the lower and middle classes under the burden of excessive taxation and labor service. Moreover, the sacrifices the imperial government demanded caused most citizens to lose interest in its preservation and turn their best efforts and hopes increasingly towards the Kingdom of Heaven. Still it would be difficult to explain why the resources of the great Greco-Roman community were so woefully inadequate, if some internal drain had not contributed to depleting its already limited reserve of strength.

Men are the prime material of history; let us look first at demography, that is, population trends. Even when Rome was in its heyday, an average life expectancy of twenty-five years was barely enough to insure a modest increase in the number of adult laborers which its economy badly needed to produce a surplus. A slight change in the proportion of births to deaths would transform the increase into a deficit; and though certain regions were overpopulated, the Empire needed all its men for the inflexible task of feeding and equipping not only the producers themselves, but also a large army and a cumbersome bureaucracy. Ever since Augustus' time, the government had taken steps to promote marriage and parenthood among Roman citizens; but children do not come by decree, and the birth rate inexorably declined. It was still lower among slaves, whose numbers could no longer be swollen through capture at war; for the early Empire was usually at peace, and the later Empire was seldom victorious. Worse still, the wars of the later Empire caused the death rate to soar, not so much on account of battlefield casualties as because they were apt to bring famine in their wake, and famine in turn exposed men to disease. At the same time, the triumph of Christianity made ecclesiastic celibacy a depressant of the birth rate.

Very probably, however, the demographic crisis had still deeper roots. The cyclical flows and ebbs of disease and famine, which can be observed over multisecular periods, seem to be connected with certain "pulsations" of climate, of which historians are just beginning to take stock. Less long and sharp than the great prehistoric alternations of glacial and interglacial periods, these pulsations have brought about, in historical times, slow yet telling changes in the average temperature and humidity of the earth. Scattered but consistent evidence indicates that the last centuries of antiquity and the first ones of the early Middle Ages were especially cold and wet. This might not in itself have been disastrous for the normally warm and dry Mediterranean world, but it made the traditional techniques of dry farming less successful and accelerated the already advanced process of erosion. It was a great shock for Rome, in the fifth century, to be sacked by the Ostrogoths; but the slow degradation of the surrounding countryside, which preceded those dramatic events, was a greater economic catastrophe. Campania was turning into a stony wilderness, Etruria into a malarial swampland. Some other regions were less affected by soil exhaustion and endemic disease, but none was spared by the dramatic succession of "pestilences" which ravaged the Greco-Roman world over and again, from the year 180 to the mid-sixth century. These periodical epidemic outbursts were probably caused by several agents, but the greatest killer undoubtedly was the bubonic plague. There have been only two multisecular periods in recorded history when the plague, normally confined to some pockets in the Far East, repeatedly spread all over the Eurasian continent: the one we have just mentioned, and the stretch between the mid-fourteenth century and the mid-seventeenth. It is probably not an accident that both periods coincided with a cold and wet pulsation of the climate.

By the fifth century of our era, when the Barbarians finally broke through the Roman defenses in the West, the population of the Empire was reduced in numbers, weakened by undernourishment, demoralized by defeat, and oppressed by overtaxation. Yet its resistance had not collapsed everywhere: the eastern half of the Empire rolled back the invaders, mended its fences, and headed for another thousand years of respectable survival. In the West, the victorious Barbarians did not deliberately set out to destroy what was left of the old order, but usually tried to patch it up in order to enjoy its advantages. The task, however, was clearly too hard for them. Their numbers were so small that the whole nation of the Ostrogoths, coming under Theodoric to conquer Italy, could shut themselves for several months within the walls of one Italian city, Pavia, and wait there for a favorable turn of the war. Above all, their political organization and technological equipment were so modest, that they were utterly incapable of arresting the decline of the ailing Roman economy. Recovery came more readily to the eastern half of the Empire—what we call the Byzantine Empire—and there the Barbarians could be of no help because they were thrown out.

In a broad sense, the barbarian age lasted until the tenth century in the parts of western Europe where the tide turned sooner, and, in other parts, until the twelfth or even the fourteenth. When it was ended, the European nations achieved something better than recovery: they produced a more dynamic economy than those of Rome and Byzantium. Unconsciously, the Barbarians prepared the ground by quickening the ruin of the old order and allowing the wreckage to disintegrate. The new order, however, was not their work but that of later generations and mixed teams.

AGRICULTURE IN THE
BARBARIAN AGE

The economic set-up of the Barbarians, both in their countries of origin and in the conquered provinces, is harder to describe than that of the Romans. Not only is information scantier, but it reveals sharp differences between coarse Saxons and comparatively refined Burgundians, between far-away Scandinavians and Visigoths camping near the Roman heart of the Empire. We shall stress the traits which were most unlike those of the Greco-Roman world, but we must not forget that the two cultures also had many points in common and drew ever closer during the long peace that followed the age of invasions and migrations.

The culture of the Barbarians was even more thoroughly rural than that of the Romans, but it was less deeply rooted in the soil. It still had a touch of nomadism, mingling agriculture proper with hunting and herding, because men did not yet fully control nature, allowed forests and waters to cover some of the best land, feared wolves and craved game. They relied less heavily than the Romans on cultivated plants and more on meat and milk; rather than striving to preserve the fertility of the soil through laborious techniques, they alternated frequently their cultivations from one field to another while letting cattle graze on a large part of their holdings. Eventually, if it was possible, they moved on to virgin land and cleared it, while allowing the forest to close in again behind them. Slash and burn agriculture (that is, cutting down trees, setting fire to the underbrush, and cultivating the ash-enriched soil until it is exhausted) yields high returns at first sowing; it was practiced in northern Russia until recently and still is widespread among underdeveloped peoples where forests are thick and land is thinly populated. This improvident, adventurous way of life, or some modifications of it, greatly increased the danger of starvation and checked the increase of the population. On the other hand, any increase had to be met either by more sparing ways to exploit the soil, or by contests with other people for a new share of the thinly settled, but not inexhaustible space. The early history of the barbarian tribes is full of clashes and pushes from end to end of the great northern European plain; the conquest of the western half of the Roman Empire is only its last chapter. Thereafter, it became indispensable for the invaders to pause and learn how to conserve the soil. Their economy of waste drew closer to the economy of saturation of the conquered people.

Conversely the Romans, whose numbers had been diminishing although they still made up the majority of the population in the former territory of the western Empire, were less and less driven to lavish labor on unrewarding soil. The trend had begun long before the fall of Rome. Soil exhaustion, heavy taxation, and insecurity conspired to make small farms unattractive. Independent peasants left their exposed land in droves, and sought shelter in the large estates (*saltus* or *villae*) where a great landowner employed great numbers of dependents to cultivate the better patches or to graze animals on the worse ones. The landowner was seldom tender-hearted, but he had to treat laborers with some consideration as labor became a scarce commodity, and he could withstand all kinds of pressure better than an ordinary peasant. It made little difference for the latter if and when a Roman master was displaced by a Barbarian; likewise, a Barbarian who had not received a large estate when settling down on Roman territory faced the same problems as a Roman small farmer, and tried to meet them in the same way. Thus, gradually, the chessboard of cultivated fields broke up, and large empty spaces surrounded the loosely exploited holdings of powerful men; trees grew again on deforested hills, brush covered the spreading marshes, and the economy of saturation came to resemble the economy of waste. The gap between Barbarian primitiveness and Roman decadence, which was shrinking in the political and intellectual fields, narrowed down in the methods of cultivation and patterns of settlement as well.

That the gap was not entirely closed depends primarily on geographic features which men cannot radically change. We have noted the main characteristics of the Mediterranean countries: a collection of small stretches of comparatively level land, hemmed in by the sea and the mountains; much sunshine, little rain, moderate seasonal variations of temperature. Continental Europe, the original home of the Barbarians, is almost exactly the opposite: an endless plain, well provided with water and ill favored by the sun, with prolonged cold winters and scorching summers. Left to itself, the heavy soil will bring forth tall trees and fodder for wild or tame animals of any kind; cultivation requires none of the ceaseless pampering demanded by the Mediterranean lean earth, but a concentrated effort with powerful tools. To some extent, this fundamental contrast was blurred by migrations of men and techniques. First, the Romans had expanded their husbandry far beyond the Mediterranean shores, in regions which had some or all of the characteristics of continental Europe: the Po Valley, northern France, England, and the Rhineland. Then, the Barbarians swarmed into the peninsulas and islands of the Mediterranean, and introduced there some of their techniques, for they were not so primitive that they had no useful agricultural practices to teach their more sophisticated neighbors. As centuries went by, the contrast between Romans and Barbarians became less significant than the geographic division between

Mediterranean and continental methods, or between northern and southern Europe—a division that does not coincide precisely with any political, national, or linguistic borders, yet still affects agriculture today.

To what extent was the agriculture of the barbarian age successful in its main tasks of feeding the laborers and producing surpluses for other consumers or reserves for lean years? The extreme poverty of information, especially for the central centuries of the barbarian age, has led some historians to cast forward the shadow of the initial, disastrous meeting of Roman decadence with German primitiveness, and to assume that things went from bad to worse ever after. This is probably an exaggeration: the diminished demographic pressure, the abandonment of much submarginal land, the disbanding of the costly administrative superstructure of the Roman Empire, the simpler though not slighter appetites of the German ruling class, and the reduced impact of war and taxation must have brought some relief. Relief, however, was bought at the price of a general lowering of standards. Governments cut down their services still faster than their demands; roads, irrigation systems, and other public works deteriorated in the formerly Roman territory and hardly existed in the other parts of western Europe; illiteracy became almost universal among laymen and far from rare among the clergy; a chronically insufficient labor force was hard put to obtain the bare necessities for themselves and a few luxuries for their coarse masters. No doubt prices during the early Middle Ages sank to an all-time low; but this was a token of monetary and economic stagnation, not a result of abundance.

In a justified reaction against a totally catastrophic interpretation of the so-called Dark Ages some modern scholars depicted barbarian Europe as a great breeding ground of technological innovations. As a matter of fact, certain new tools and techniques that contributed significantly to the European recovery from the tenth century on may be traced back to the barbarian period (or even earlier); but their diffusion or their impact cannot possibly have been great in an age that is otherwise represented by the extant sources as utterly depopulated and depressed. A few figures on the yield of cereals tell the story with terrible eloquence. Under the late Roman Republic and early Empire, the average yield in the Italian peninsula was four times the seed, with peak harvests above ten times the seed in the better soils of Sicily and Tuscany; much later, in thirteenth-century England, a threefold yield was regarded as unprofitable unless prices were unusually inflated; but in the Carolingian period, which was probably the high point of the barbarian age, the largest harvests on record were just above twice the seed, the lowest ones fell below one and a half times the seed. This means that at least one half of the cultivated area served merely to produce seed. No doubt hunting, fishing, dairy products, and vegetables grown in well-manured backyards supplemented the diet; but it is no wonder that in a society where bread was so scarce and uncertain the term "keeper of loaves," *hlaford,* came to mean, in Anglo-Saxon, "master," or *lord.*

Yet we must also keep in mind that the barbarian age brought about some equalization among the ill-nourished people of the lower classes. Ancient Rome had richer aristocrats and more comfortable free farmers, but was beset by landless proletarians and depended on slave labor. Whether rich or poor, all free citizens were equal before the law, but slaves were cattle at the mercy of their master. The long depression of the barbarian age fostered the growth of an intermediate group, made up of degraded freemen and promoted slaves, all of whom were substantially free in their relations with third parties but unfree in their relations with a master or lord. The new social group, which eventually inherited the old name of the slaves (*servi,* serfs), also absorbed many able-bodied proletarians. At the bottom of society there only remained a dwindling number of unenfranchised slaves and disabled or idle beggars. This complex evolution, which began before the fall of Rome and was protracted into the later Middle Ages but took its longest stride in the barbarian period, cannot be described in detail here. Let us note, however, that its fundamental causes were the demographic depression and the lack of physical and economic security. Insecurity, as we have seen, forced the humbler freemen to submit or "recommend" (*commendare*) themselves to stronger and richer people. Scarcity of manpower eliminated involuntary unemployment and forced slave owners to improve the lot of their human cattle in order to make them more resistant and willing to work. Some historians also ascribe an important role to the preaching of the

Church, but this is debatable. No doubt Christianity promises the
Kingdom of Heaven to the submissive and proclaims all souls equal
before God, but organized religion is seldom revolutionary on earth,
and practical ethics does not so much determine practical economics
as it adjusts to it.

Be that as it may, this much is sure: the barbarian age tarnished
the luster of the upper class and debased the living standard of
most of the people, but it had work for every able-bodied man. In
moral terms, it may be argued whether a more equally shared
misery is better or worse than a diversified profile of riches and
poverty. In economic terms, a low platform may serve for the
launching of economic growth, but this cannot occur without the
injection of some powerful driving force, and no such force is visible
anywhere before the tenth century.

THE TRADES IN THE
BARBARIAN AGE

The predominance of agriculture over all other occupations became crushing in the barbarian age. Food surpluses were too small
to support a substantial number of people who did not produce
and gather their share; the privileged few who had both food and
money to spare usually had robust appetites but small interest in
the refinements of life, and kept their treasures idle in their coffers
or froze them in readily enjoyable jewelry rather than investing
them in business ventures. This, more than any substantial outflow
of precious metals towards the richer countries beyond western
Europe, accounts for the fact that prices tumbled down in the midst
of scarcity of most goods and services, and coinage was reduced to a
trickle of coins with the highest purchasing power, while the smaller
denominations used in daily transactions gradually disappeared.
People normally endeavored to produce (or have produced by their
dependents) nearly all they needed. What small transactions still
occurred, and many larger ones, could be carried out by exchanging
one good for another (such goods might range in value from a loaf
of bread or a cupful of grain to an estate with its cattle and serfs);

money was used exceptionally for large purchases and for the storing of wealth.

This general picture, however, must be enriched with many nuances. It is virtually impossible to distinguish one chronological period from another in the agricultural history of the barbarian age, because agriculture changes but slowly, and produces very few quantitative records, most of which are significant only for the specific territory from which they come. It is a little less difficult to take guesses at the evolution of commerce and the crafts. Yet even there, the sustained and learned debate that has engrossed the attention of economic historians for almost fifty years is now dying out without any general agreement. The basic argument concerned a comparative assessment of the first and second halves of the Barbarian Age: in France, the Merovingian and the Carolingian periods; in Italy, the Lombard and the Carolingian; in England, the early and the late Anglo-Saxon; and so forth. Before the discussion started, it was taken for granted that decline had been continuous during the first half, with a low point in all economic activities other than sustenance agriculture by the seventh or early eighth century, and that the Carolingians in the late eighth and early ninth centuries had brought about a revival, unfortunately nipped in the bud by the collapse of their empire and the subsequent wave of invasions. This profile, however, was not based on quantitative data on commerce and industry in the two periods (especially for the first one there are none that can be of much help), but mainly on the assumption that economic trends ran parallel to better known trends in literacy and literature, art and philosophy, government and war. Such an assumption deserved to be challenged and it was, even to the extent of reversing the diagnosis and pronouncing the Carolingian period an economic low point after a not too unsuccessful Merovingian, Lombard, or early Anglo-Saxon period. More evidence was dug out, but none of it was conclusive, and the revision elicited a number of counter-revisions.

We still lack quantitative data and the debate is moot. But it has served at least two useful purposes. On the one hand, we have been reminded that the evolution of crafts and, above all, that of international commerce are linked to international events. As a matter of fact, the changing relations of the West with Byzantium, the surge of Islam in the seventh century, and its consolidation over the southern half of the Mediterranean world (from Syria to Spain) had European repercussions that we can no longer neglect. On the other hand, attention has been attracted to the difference between an early period, when the Roman legacy had not been totally dispersed but adjustment to changed conditions had not really begun, and a late period, when Rome was merely a distant memory but a new economic formula was slowly emerging. It matters little that we cannot tell which of the two periods was slightly better than the other, for both of them were fundamentally depressed.

Geographically, too, there were disparities which partly coincided with the north-south partition we noted in agriculture, but went deeper and included more local variations. In Italy a debased tradition of urban life and activities survived the first Barbarian conquest by the Ostrogoths and the "Roman" reconquest by Justinian, the famous Byzantine emperor of the sixth century. Soon after, the Lombards occupied the larger part of the country but were to some extent infected by the habits of the areas still held in the name of Byzantium; and even Charlemagne's Franks when in Rome had to do like the Romans. Thus a tenuous but unbroken thread connected the ancient Italian city with the late medieval one. In Spain also there was no total eclipse between the waning town life of the Visigoths and the waxing life introduced by the Arab conquerors. Indeed, the whole Mediterranean facade of western Europe benefited from relations with the Byzantine and Islamic worlds, and sharply contrasted with the isolation of the countrified hinterland.

A more modest kind of trade, ruder crafts, and more primitive towns also began to appear during the barbarian age along the other "Mediterranean" formed by the North Sea and the Baltic Sea: the Frisians, the Anglo-Saxons, the Scandinavians, and the Rhinish Germans competed for the opportunities arising along the frontier between half-civilized Barbarians and uncivilized ones, often alternating trade with agriculture, piracy, and war. Some commerce also was possible inside western and central Europe, wherever a monastery or an episcopal see established a group of potential consumers, or an unusually sophisticated lord was not content with what his serfs could make for him. In the larger part

of Europe, however, the visitations of trade tended to be as unexpected as famines, plagues, and invasions; as a matter of fact,
these calamities drove holes into the thin armor of countrified self-
sufficiency, and then the not-always-available help of an international merchant (often, a Jewish one) was the only alternative to
starvation. But there also were more pleasant windfalls, such as the
appearance of a peddler on a feast day; and even the most backward village had to buy salt if it could not obtain it otherwise.

We must beware of overestimating the size of commerce in the
barbarian age: even at the best moments and in the most lively
places, it was very small. Industrial activity must have been still
smaller, apart from the low grade crafts that are the indispensable
complement of country life: ordinary smithery and carpentry, coarse
pottery and weaving, and other types of production meant primarily
for immediate use on the spot and not for sale on the market. But
we must beware even more of dismissing what market economy
there was as a negligible quantity. In a still atmosphere the softest
breeze matters. We often hear, in early medieval sources, of "large"
cities, "rich" merchants, "famous" smiths: that is what they looked
like in the context of the time. Just as slaves were slightly upgraded
because they were getting rare, so did skilled workers and merchants
cut a more respectable figure than their better equipped but more
commonplace Roman predecessors. Many of them, it is true, shared
the fate of the great majority of freemen, forced to recommend
themselves to a powerful lord; but others maintained their independence, and some gained acceptance into the higher ranks of
society. The most striking case in point is that of the moneyers
(manufacturers of coins), who rose from the unenviable condition
of hard-driven workmen in the Roman imperial mints to that of
independent entrepreneurs or high officials of the barbarian governments. Their numbers, productivity and skill had fallen far
below those of their Roman predecessors; but the maker and han-
dler of money had become an important personage when coins
were scarce and credit hard to obtain.

These hopeful signs, however, were more than offset by the agricultural, military, and religious shape of the barbarian society. The
western Church upbraided the quest for wealth, of which the merchant seemed the most typical representative, and bolstered the

rational arguments of the ancient philosophers against the money
lender with a moral condemnation of interest charges as sins against
charity. Among influential laymen there were not many intellec-
tuals or civil servants who could mitigate the instinctive contempt
of the upper class for any member of society who did not normally
fight or hunt. Even in the largest and best managed estates which
were geared for the production of a salable surplus and collected
modest dues in cash from tenants, the golden rule was seeing to it
that "it should not be necessary to request or buy anything from
outside." Without the stimulating medium of substantial towns,
merchants and craftsmen had to seek their customers in a myriad
of unreceptive rural mansions and hamlets, and could not easily
enlarge their operations and grow rich enough to command respect.

CATHOLIC EUROPE AND
HER NEIGHBORS

Of all the changes that the barbarian age brought to the Greco-
Roman world the most clear-cut and irreversible was the change
of geographical frameworks. In three successive stages, the Mediterranean community gave way to new political, intellectual, and economic constellations. First the collapse of the Roman protective
barriers in the West enabled the Barbarians not only to lower the
cultural level of the conquered countries but also to raise slowly
the level of their native lands. Then Byzantium found it impossible
to keep its higher, more conservative civilization firmly in touch
with the interbred civilization of the West. Lastly, the Arabs sub-
merged more than one half of the Mediterranean territories and
established there an original blend of the Greco-Roman and Persian cultures with their own. Thus, by the time of Charlemagne,
the sea that had functioned as the central highway of the Greco-
Roman community became the border between three different communities, which in the lack of an appropriate economic term may
be identified through their predominant religions: Islamic, Ortho-
dox, and Catholic. Their centers of gravity were far apart: Baghdad,
the capital of the caliphs, was a stepping stone to inner Asia; Constantinople was the gateway to the Black Sea and Asia Minor;

Aachen, closer to what we have called "the northern Mediterranean" than to the classic Mediterranean, indicated the northern and Germanic interests of the Carolingians. Nevertheless, the three communities had not entirely turned their back on the old Roman sea, nor had they broken all relations with one another. Before leaving the barbarian age, we must take a brief look at the economy of the two great neighbors of the emerging Catholic Europe.

Byzantium was the political continuation of the late Roman Empire in the east, on a territory which alternatively expanded and contracted with the fortune of war but always loomed large as compared to the petty barbarian states. Her basic economic assets and liabilities also bore a Roman stamp: on the active side of the balance, a skillful agriculture of the intensive Mediterranean type, a diversified industry, an active commerce based on cash and to a smaller amount on credit, a good number of easily accessible towns; on the passive side, high taxation, little mechanization, and deep-rooted biases against nonagricultural pursuits. The favorable characteristics, however, were enfeebled because Byzantium had smaller resources than Rome, was seldom at peace, and could not entirely escape the agents of depression that affected more severely the barbarian West. The population diminished, its culture declined, its composition changed as many Barbarians were admitted as colonists or allowed to stay in territories temporarily lost to them. Most towns survived, and so did the opposite poles of the lower classes (slaves, and the poorer free men), but few cities thrived and an intermediate status similar to Western serfdom made its appearance. Like their Roman predecessors (but unlike most barbarian kings) the Byzantine emperors felt responsible for the welfare of their subjects, but their means were inadequate and their frequent interventions in economic affairs were often unfair or unwise. More important still, the very fact that economic conditions had not intolerably worsened encouraged conservatism where innovation would have been useful. Nevertheless, there were valuable novelties, especially in shipbuilding, commercial practices, and the luxury industries of silk and glass. Above all, whatever was preserved of the ancient economic organization was easily enough to keep Byzantium far ahead of the Catholic West until the tenth century at least.

The economy of Islam defies summary description: the central caliphate and the splinter states that began to emerge in the late eighth century embraced the most diverse lands, peoples, and traditions. Moreover, the sparse sources of the early Islamic period are barely beginning to attract the expert attention that economic historians have long been devoting to Latin and Greek sources. It is beyond doubt that the Arab conquest brought dividends soon after the initial destruction; there was hardly a "barbarian" interlude comparable to the long depression of the West. In the Sasanian (Persian) Empire, which they swallowed whole, and in Syria, Egypt, and Northwest Africa, which they wrested from Byzantium, the Arabs inherited going, if not thriving economies, and absorbed the techniques of two mature civilizations. The amalgamation under one flag of all that territory, plus the Iberian peninsula, a large proportion of Central Asia, some parts of India, and, of course, Arabia, engendered new potential for growth, but growth was not easy in the presence of the adverse demographic and economic trends we have noted in Catholic Europe and Byzantium. These trends, we may now add, seem to have occurred in all other parts of the Old World for which any economic evidence is available, such as pre-Islamic Persia and post-Han China, though timing and intensity varied to some extent.

There are reasons to believe that in the Islamic world as a whole the cycle ran about a hundred years ahead of Catholic Europe. By the tenth century, when Europe was just getting out of depression, some Muslim countries were well on the way to their medieval peak. Their growth had almost everywhere stopped or slowed down by the end of the twelfth century, while Catholic Europe was only approaching her zenith. On the other hand, even at its highest point the economic growth of Islam was not much greater than that of Byzantium and definitely smaller than that of the late medieval West. The Arabian Nights are fascinating but misleading; they see Baghdad in the age of Harun al-Rashid through a magnifying glass. Actually most roads were poor or nonexistent, ships were small, coinage was barely adequate, and the conspicuous consumption of a few rich people did not make up for the destitution of the masses. Because nomadic grazing and caravan trade had been the basic occupations in their country of origin, the Arabs tended to despise farming and respected traveling commerce, the profession of Mohammed himself. But although this unusual bent could provide a fresh stimulus to economic growth, it was partly offset by the Arabs' traditional disinclination for political order and teamwork. These contradictory drives, moreover, were braked by the reemerging biases of the conquered Persian, Byzantine, and Spanish upper classes, who lived in cities but had always looked down on trade. Nevertheless, in the early Middle Ages the economic pace of the Islamic world was distinctly faster than that of Catholic Europe, if only because it drew its resources and techniques from an incomparably larger range of lands and cultures.

Unquestionably, the Muslim and Byzantine experiences could and did transmit precious teachings to Catholic Europe. We shall indicate, in due time, the principal elements that added power to the European awakening from the tenth century on. Many other borrowings are attested by the Arab or Greek etymologies of a large number of economic terms in the vocabulary of every west European language. In the Barbarian period, however, Europe was unprepared to learn, and her more advanced neighbors felt no urge to teach. This does not mean that communication was absolutely impossible: both the Byzantine and the Muslims welcomed strangers who would contribute ideas, manpower, and commodities; Islam in its early centuries was particularly tolerant of foreign religions. Without being always intolerant, the barbarian states of western Europe were more provincial (or, rather, tribal); some Saxon and Anglo-Saxon laws took for granted that a stranger for whom nobody would vouch should be sold as a slave or treated as a thief. In spite of these extreme statements, however, aliens traveled to and fro under the protection of a royal safeconduct or a pilgrim's garb, periodical markets offered privileged meeting grounds, and many semiautonomous seaports, especially in Italy, were open to trade with both friendly and unfriendly foreign countries.

To this we shall return later; but we must stress at once that whereas the impact of economic and cultural exchanges with the Islamic world was usually limited by mutual incomprehension, friction with Byzantium was less of an obstacle to communication and grudging admiration. Very likely the balance of trade of Catholic Europe (if we may use such a prestigious term for a trickle of goods) was more favorable in the relations with the Islamic countries. They provided a practically inexhaustible market for European heavy raw materials (timber, iron, copper) and slaves, while selling to Europe a modest amount of spices and luxury goods. But it is doubtful whether an underdeveloped country gains more by what it exports than by what it imports. Though Byzantium bought little from Catholic Europe and was a constant source of irritation as a wayward, yet more successful sister, it was to her that Westerners turned first when they looked for refined wares, artistic know-how, and economic or political models that were not available at home. Paradoxically, imitation became indispensable when the Carolingians, after unifying most of the Barbarian states, claimed back the Roman primogeniture that had passed on to Constantinople and endeavored to set up a western Empire that would match or outdo Byzantium. Though Charlemagne was deeply attached to German customs and Roman devotion, he and his immediate successors were gradually driven to look abroad for a model of imperial organization. The Byzantine Empire was the only suitable model they could find.

In the economic field, the Carolingians strove, with a stronger religious undertone and a weaker or hazier technique of enforcement, to pursue much the same aims as their eastern imperial rivals. With a somewhat cross-eyed look at earthly power and eternal salvation, they forbade the smuggling of Christian slaves, arms, and other essential materials into foreign territory, they organized and supervised markets for internal trade, restricted or entirely outlawed "usurious" interest, and tried to reach a uniform, stable system of weights, measures, coins, and prices. They did succeed in establishing a fixed proportion of weights, reflected in the ponderal and monetary equivalence of a pound to 20 shillings and 240 deniers; that equivalence survived, in England at least, down to our days, but its main purpose was flouted by the decline of the actual weight and alloy quality of coins and the fluctuations of prices. Still, had the Carolingian Empire endured, Catholic Europe might perhaps have become a centralized, authoritarian, land-rooted monarchy combining Byzantine with Barbarian characteristics. It crumbled before the end of the ninth century, and the budding nations of the West were released to work their way up by trial and error, in an original key.

2

The Growth of
Self-Centered Agriculture

THE TURN OF THE
DEMOGRAPHIC TIDE

Manpower was the essential asset and motor in the lightly mechanized economy of the ancient world. Its scarcity and diminished skill became a dominant problem of the barbarian age. We cannot be surprised if the revival and soaring of the later Middle Ages coincided with a resumption of population growth accompanied by a resurgence of skill.

When did the demographic tide turn? The beginnings are hidden in the least documented centuries of the barbarian age. It takes time before the growth of a small quantity snowballs to noticeable size. Although we cannot be reasonably sure before the tenth century that in a large part of Catholic Europe the vicious circle of low population, low production, and low consumption was broken, we cannot rule out the possibility that change began somewhat earlier. We do hear, in the Carolingian age, of new villages being founded, woods being cleared, and settlers being attracted by monasteries, castles, and other sheltered places. Such fragmentary evidence, however, can be interpreted in more than one way: monastic and seigniorial agglomerations may grow at the expense of unprotected centers; clearings may accommodate people who have abandoned exhausted fields elsewhere; new villages may disappear soon after they have been established. It may be somewhat safer to refer to

27

the record of two major factors affecting the demographic trends, climate and plagues. The last of the catastrophic pestilences that swept through the Eurasian continent took place in 742–43. Later sources still mention epidemics of various kinds, but not before the Black Death of the mid-fourteenth century do we encounter calamities of major spread and proportions. Information on climate is less reliable because it is available only at a few widely separate places, and because changes in climate do not affect all places equally. Still the little we know about the normally cold regions in the far north of Europe and the adjacent seas indicates a warm "pulsation" that began in the ninth century or slightly earlier and made the great Scandinavian migrations possible at latitudes previously obstructed by ice. In the ninth century, too, we come across the first definite tokens of crowding in two districts where the fertility of the land and the presence of an important city created a favorable conjuncture: the Parisian area and the surroundings of Milan. One wonders whether this incipient but localized growth had a bearing on the so-called Carolingian renaissance, whose achievements, remarkable though they were, affected only a small minority of the people and were mixed with signs of economic discomfort and technological inadequacy.

Be that as it may, the Carolingian Empire was soon brought down by the high mortality rate of its latter rulers, the weakness of its internal structure, and a sudden resumption of barbarian invasions. It would be tempting to ascribe the invasions to the hunger for land of nations swollen by population growth, but we never hear of large numbers. There is no positive reason to explain the new round differently from the earlier drives of Germans, Huns, and Arabs on the civilized world: no special demographic pressure is necessary for seminomadic people to reach for ill-defended grass beyond the fence rather than nurse their own meadow. As a matter of fact, the Scandinavians who carried out ubiquitous raids in western Europe, made a dazzling career in Russia, colonized Iceland and Greenland, and touched America by the year 1000, were Germans of the outer fringe. The Slavs who pushed relentlessly westwards on a long front were only cousins of the Germans, but their customs were not very different from those of the early Goths and Franks. The Magyars who entrenched themselves in the Danubian region belonged to the same uncouth family as the Huns, scourge of the late Roman Empire. The Muslims of various provenances who conquered the major islands of the Mediterranean from Sicily to Cyprus and carried further north their razzias for slaves and other booty were the descendants (some of their fellow citizens said, "the dregs") of the larger and more spirited hosts that had created the Arab caliphate. What was new about the new invaders was not their demographic or economic stature, but the texture of their target: no longer a majestic if decadent empire like Rome, Byzantium or Persia, but a half-barbarian empire (or the equally semibarbarous kingdoms that coexisted with it or arose from its disintegration) which could hardly bring together its local deputies and plug the gaps of a sparsely inhabited frontier. Both the attacks and the defense were discontinuous and flexible; there was no capital or central arsenal whose fall might deliver an entire country into the hands of a determined enemy, but an endless succession of mediocre castles, monasteries, and self-contained settlements. All this made penetration easy and conquest slippery; it also shortened the time needed for reconstruction, whether the Barbarians were ultimately ousted, absorbed, or accepted as masters.

The invasions and the political disorders did not seriously interfere with the flow of the demographic tide. By the tenth century, the signs were clear and unmistakable: the population was growing. Moreover, it tended to leave the more isolated locations for larger villages and towns. This, at the beginning, was more often an answer to insecurity in the open country than an indication that agriculture was making more room for urbanized nonagricultural pursuits. Eventually, however, commerce and industry were bound to benefit by the process. Even by the most lavish standards of settlement, there was no dearth of unoccupied space for cultivation. It took many generations before the sustained demographic growth supplied the manpower needed to eliminate the wide uninhabited stretches which made communications difficult, organization spotty, and food supply inadequate. And though there is record, sooner or later, of cvercrowding and overcropping in some regions, at other places there still were underpopulated areas and unreclaimed (but not unreclaimable) districts in the fourteenth century, when the long period of demographic growth came to a full stop. In the most

literal sense, at no time in the Middle Ages was the wolf kept away
from every door. No doubt agricultural underpopulation is not a
rigid factor: the optimum density varies according to the nature
of the soil, the quality of tools and techniques, and the amount of
surplus allotted for the support of nonagricultural people. But
these variables in turn are not unelastic: an increased concentration
of labor may improve the land, multiply the tools, ameliorate the
techniques, and stimulate nonagricultural activities. In our own
days the Israelis have shown how the immigration of intelligent,
resolute people can transform a desert into a thriving landscape sup-
porting large cities. Not without reason medieval writers tended to
regard a dense rural population as a prime indication of general
prosperity: in the larger part of Catholic Europe, the initial move
towards economic growth was made by men determined to re-create
their own landscape.

PATTERNS OF AGRICULTURAL
EXPANSION

Anyone who has tried to cultivate his backyard—to say nothing
of larger spaces—knows the infinite diversity of challenge and response within the same plot. Multiply this by the surface of Europe,
the span of centuries, the differences among individuals and people
in an age of imperfect communication, then consider that most of
the record is lost (actually, more often than not it was never com-
piled) and that what little remains has only begun to be studied,
and you will realize the impossibility to describe the local manifestations of the agricultural expansion between the tenth and the
fourteenth century. We can surmise the general trend, but we have
hardly any figures to measure it before the late twelfth century.
When figures begin to appear, they are so scattered in time and
space that any averaging of them is bound to be misleading. With
these warnings in mind, we still find it necessary to inscribe tenta-
tively a few details in our inevitably oversimplified contour map.

Details, indeed, are the core of reality in the tenth century and
most of the eleventh, when virtually all efforts, whether economic,
intellectual, or military, were discontinuous, circumscribed, unco-

ordinated, and often at cross purposes with other efforts. The failure of the Carolingian attempt at harnessing the whole of Catholic Europe under a joint political and ecclesiastic leadership uncovered the flimsiness of the underpinnings of the restored "Roman Empire" in the West. No alternative solution on a more than local or, at most, regional scale was in sight. There followed a protracted period of confusion and struggle: at one time or another every social group, every village, every family had to fight for property, liberty, and physical survival not only against foreign invaders but also against their closest neighbors. It is not surprising that the voices reaching us from that period are full of distress and frustration; the more so, as most of them come from monasteries, churches, royal officers, and other beneficiaries of the old order, whose holdings were choice targets for the depredations of the new barbarians, the usurpations of ruthless lords and adventurers, and the uprisings of dissatisfied tenants and serfs. Later historians, who accepted these sources less uncritically, have described the tenth and early eleventh centuries as an age of localism and revolution, the thorny but not unsuccessful beginning of a great revival. No doubt law and order have certain plain advantages; but the law of the barbarian age was crude and ineffective, and the Carolingian order, for all its lofty religious ideals, would have frozen the immense majority of the population under the unmovable control of a privileged few. We read something different in the forecast gloomily enounced by Agnellus of Ravenna, an ecclesiastic writer of the Carolingian decadence: "Slaves shall marry the daughters of their lord, and the lowly shall marry the noble, and from those born of impurity there shall come judges and dukes, and they shall overturn the earth." To the extent that the prophecy came true, it means that Catholic Europe moved from stagnation at the lowest level to a social and economic mobility full of dangers but open to hope.

At first, the dangers seemed to overshadow the hope. Not all the overflow of the population went to activate new and promising land. Some people were abducted or sold abroad as slaves, others were killed by war or famine before they could durably win over fresh soil, many were needed merely to repopulate areas that had just been laid waste. But enslavement, warfare, and starvation were nothing new, and there already had been vacant homesteads (*mansi absi*) in the midst of otherwise thickly settled Carolingian estates. The difference is that from the tenth century on net gains exceeded losses and tended to stick, no matter whether agricultural expansion was promoted by a monastery deploying its serfs on its property, or by a warrior enlarging his grip around a conquered stronghold, or by a peasant community encroaching on seigniorial preserves, or by a frontiersman venturing out in the wild. We shall never know who were the most effective promoters in the early period: it is relatively easy to follow the activity of an ecclesiastical institution, which usually wrote down its exploits, but much harder to assess the achievements of squatters, who became reluctantly vocal only when their claims were challenged. There are lands which seem to have been settled, abandoned, and settled again more than once, and one cannot always tell whether the intervals correspond to a failure of the colonizing attempt, a predictable move of seminomadic cultivators, or a prolonged rest granted to the soil by people who do not yet know how to maintain its fertility. Sometimes we have to wait many decades before knowing for sure that a certain territory has been permanently annexed to the developed portion.

The patterns of settlement are as diversified as the agents, but we can single out prevalent regional trends, usually determined by a combination of factors: physical environment, ethnic tradition, and historical circumstances. "Prevalent," of course, does not mean "omnipresent"; we still are oversimplifying.

The rugged individualism of the people, the basic harshness of the soil and climate, and a sudden improvement of the latter between the late ninth century and the late eleventh gave wings to the Scandinavian expansion without altering substantially its primitive characteristics. At the beginning, agriculture proper and village settlements played a significant if modest role only in the Danish islands and in some stretches of what is today southern Sweden. In the rest of Scandinavia an extremely sparse population lived by fishing, hunting, and, above all, stock raising. We are told that Ottar, the northern Norwegian who explored the White Sea and befriended King Alfred the Great, owned twenty cows, twenty swine, twenty sheep, and no less than 600 reindeer. Some of his fellow countrymen won glory, gold, and power by raiding, trading, conquering, and settling down in Russia, northwestern Europe, and even some regions of the Mediterranean; but their economic contribution (positive or negative) soon became indistinguishable from that of the much larger population already living and working there. The Scandinavian mark was more deeply etched in Iceland, which they colonized between 874 and 930; in Greenland, their next springboard; not, however, in Newfoundland. Iceland before their coming had been known as "the desert in the Ocean," and Greenland was almost unoccupied, but "Vinland" (Newfoundland?) was sparsely inhabited by natives who drove the Norsemen off and left America for rediscovery to Columbus. It is amazing that a handful of pioneers, with rudimentary tools and no navigational instruments, could go that far; more amazing that they chose to settle down and farm in such inhospitable lands while there still was room in Scandinavia, and while softer countries further south invited many of their brothers. It is true that fishing and lumbering were of great help, more so than in the motherland. But we must not underestimate the appeal of empty expanses on men unwilling to bow to a common discipline. And though the loosely organized republic of Iceland never really throve, it nurtured a brilliant literature; back at home the Scandinavians gradually organized polities similar to the older ones of Catholic Europe, but the age of adventure faded into both economic and cultural mediocrity.

Let us now move, for the sake of contrast, to the sun-drenched shores of the Mediterranean. In a large part of northern and central Italy, the ingenious work of Roman agriculturists and the chessboard plan of fields designed by Roman agrimensors had never entirely disappeared; nor had the skills of classic farming been cast totally aside. Centuries of desertion and neglect had their redeeming feature in the fact that exhausted soil had recovered its fertility and deforested mountains had regained their mantle. Nevertheless it took much courage and industry for the Italians from the tenth century on (and in some cases as early as the eighth) to reclaim the land, drain the marshes, restore the irrigation works, defy foreign raiders and, only too often, native robbers of every class and status. The ensuing agricultural redevelopment did not merely reconstruct the classic agricultural landscape, but modified it in many ways and brought under culture much ground that had seemed too swampy or too steep to the Romans. To encourage resettlement and stimulate improvements, whoever owned the land had to meet the peasants half way. There were long leases, sharecropping agreements, premiums of various kinds for anyone who would plant vines and olive or chestnut trees. Peasant communities argued endlessly with a bishop, an abbot, a count about their rights, their dues, their share in the common pastures, the borders of individual plots. In many cases, however, there could be no argument because the peasants had a written title in their hands. Literacy, if not literature, contributed to the recovery in another way: Latin manuals of agriculture were copied in monasteries, and served as primers of husbandry in the land for which they had originally been written. Freedom was less full than in the Scandinavian outposts, but it was more clearly defined; and no peasant had to fend for himself in loneliness, none forgot that if he did not like his lot he could usually look for another lord or a town that would welcome his services. Indeed, rural and urban growth were at all times closely interdependent.

The Scandinavian pattern is an extreme example of agricultural expansion into virgin land; the Italian, an extreme example of agricultural comeback in land rejuvenated by a long hibernation. Between the extremes there was room for infinite nuances. The early stages of the Christian reconquest in the Iberian peninsula led to colonization and reclamation by farmers who initially enjoyed still greater liberties than those of Italy; but the new input of labor and skill did not quite balance the exodus of many Muslim farmers, who had previously carried out a reclamation of their own. Southern France on the whole resembled Italy and Spain, but things changed rapidly as one moved farther north. Although certain by-products of the Roman colonization never lost favor in Merovingian France and its enlarged successor, the Carolingian Empire—the vine, for instance, gained ground both before and after the tenth century—the pattern of recovery was largely shaped by barbarian or, at least, medieval practices. Large estates usually applied to newly gained areas the same type of collective agriculture and spaced settlement as before (though they improved their techniques and reduced the spaces), and tried as best they could to absorb whatever was left of small independent farming. Small tenants and serfs, on the other hand, inched forward mainly by the primitive method of "assarts," that is, by clearing small wooded stretches around the corner while the lord was not looking, burning the underbrush, and starting culture with the hope that their claim would be recognized. Much the same can be said about England, but here the barbarian coloring was stronger, if only because the superficially Romanized natives had been largely driven out by the Anglo-Saxons and, later, also by Danes. Farmers gained ground, but so did sheep, which were the special asset of the country, and hunting continued to be an important source of food for lord and peasant alike.

At the same time, the outer ring of Catholic Europe expanded as the new barbarian invaders settled down and took their place in the family of organized societies. Apprenticeship was shorter because the cultural difference between them and the half-barbarian peoples of post-Carolingian Europe was smaller than that between the Barbarians of old and the inhabitants of the late Roman Empire. The Frisians and the Saxons had already been incorporated into the Carolingian Empire; under the combined influence of missionaries, soldiers, and rulers coming from the old provinces they gave up their wild anarchic tendencies and took over most of the agricultural practices and organization of northern France. By the late tenth century the Frisians were actively participating in the reclamation of coastal marshes that went on from the mouth of the Rhine to that of the Loire, while the Saxons were applying to the western Slavs the lessons they had been forced to learn from the Carolingians. (The further expansion of German agriculture will be described later.) The Slavs, in turn, had long lived in villages and practiced agriculture at a level but slightly inferior to that of the Saxons; some of their tools and plants were better, and contributed to the progress of western agriculture. The Magyars did not shed readily their nomadic habits—we are told that as late as the twelfth century they spent much time under tents—but they welcomed foreign influences. "Immigrants," says one of their earliest books, "bring in different languages, customs, tools, and weapons. This diversity is an ornament for the realm, a decoration for the court, and an object of fear for our enemies." Only the Irish, in spite of their early adoption of Christianity and their remarkable artistic development in pre-Carolingian times, remained almost impenetrable to foreign custom. For unaccounted reasons, probably rooted in social custom, they continued to cherish isolated farmsteads and to raid one another's cattle. Thus they missed almost entirely the economic growth sweeping the rest of Europe, and ultimately they lost even their rugged independence.

CHANGES IN THE DIETS
AND THE CROPS

The growth of the population and the extension of the cultivated area forced Catholic Europe out of the contracted stability where it might have indefinitely lingered. They could not, however, automatically insure economic growth. The survival of a larger number, if it is not accompanied by a proportionally increased per capita productivity, may pull a civilization downward: Egypt, India, Java, and China are modern examples, whereas Japan and a large part of the Western world exemplify the opposite process of productivity increasing faster than population and space under culture. It is true that space is finally inelastic. We are now facing a new threat, that of crowding the earth beyond the limit of physical comfort. This problem, however, had no urgency for the medieval man. Within the fences of his village or the walls of his town the air might be full of stench, the water unclean, the neighbors too close, the living quarters cramped; his ability to move might be restricted by law or impeded by insecurity; but he did not live on an overcrowded planet. Food production was the basic problem, to an extent that we cannot easily grasp in the affluent society of our day, even though hunger is not unknown in our United States, and though every year countless thousands of people still die of hunger or malnutrition in other parts of the world.

Famines, that is, acute and widespread outbursts of hunger, are recorded more consistently than ordinary malnutrition in the sources of a chronically undernourished society. The fact that mentions do not become more frequent in the records of the tenth and early eleventh century, though both the number of people and that of extant sources steadily increase, is an indirect testimony to the success of agriculture—and also to the improvement of communications, which enhances the mobility of food and people in and out of the most stricken districts. By the early thirteenth century, large-scale famines became quite rare. But that does not mean that malnutrition had been conquered. The obstacle was not only quantitative but also qualitative: there was no clear knowledge of the elements that go into a balanced diet, but only an intuitive selection based on experience and, above all, availability. Needless to say, what was available to the lord was not necessarily available to the serf. One fact is certain: in the form of bread, porridge, or mush, cereals were almost everywhere the basis of human alimentation, in the middle ages as in classic antiquity—so much so that in low Latin and some of the vernaculars everything else is called *companaticum*, "accompaniment of bread." This took care of carbohydrates; the intake of proteins and vitamins was skimpier. Happily, milk with its byproducts was available throughout Catholic Europe, but it was very important only among herdsmen. Fresh fruit played a significant role in the south, meat was less sparingly consumed in the north, fish was helpful wherever sea or fresh water was not too far, eggs were ubiquitous. The migrations of the barbarian age blurred but did not abolish the partitions between the areas of olive oil and lard or butter, and those of wine and beer; either wine or beer were well nigh indispensable where water was unsafe. Leguminous and green plants were useful supplements to the diet. Roots were consumed out of necessity, but they were usually regarded as only one notch higher than grass, the ultimate resort in time of famine; subsisting on roots only was, together with chastity, the great exploit of hermits and saints.

Let us fill in this sketchy, static food map with a few details, and observe the details in the background of medieval change. Cereals had the lead: there were no radical innovations in the cultivated varieties, but the shifting preferences for one or another variety reflected significant changes in tastes, techniques, and standards of living. The Romans gave the highest priority to soft wheat (*triticum vulgare,* an ill-suited scientific name for the finest type of grain), which makes the best white bread. Coarser cereals such as spelt and other husked wheats, millet, and barley were raised chiefly for the use of animals, though slaves and poor country people also ate them; rye and oats were known as weeds or, at best, fodder crops. But both rye and oats resist cold climates better than does soft wheat and do not demand as much care. The Barbarians spread their cultivation and gave them a prominent place in human consumption, while sharing barley and spelt with animals and using both barley and oats for brewing a beer as thick as soup. Beer, it must be noted, was the outstanding barbarian contribution to the diet. Then, from the tenth century on, soft wheat gradually regained first place, first for the rich, then for the middle class, lastly for lower class people. It did not, however, displace the other grains, which still were good enough for less discriminating palates and for fodder, and could be sown in seasons or soils where soft wheat would not succeed. As for rice, the only important medieval addition to the family of Europe's culti-vated cereals, it was introduced to Spain and Sicily by the Arabs but played no significant role elsewhere before the early Renaissance; this was a pity, because its food value is higher than that of wheat.

Qualities of cereals, however, were less important than quantities. Although overall figures are lacking, we know for sure that total production increased continuously and rapidly between the tenth century and the thirteenth; so did per capita production, but at a slower pace because the population also was growing. The increases should be linked to three factors: the surface under cultivation, the yield, and the rotation of crops. The expansion of the cultivated area defies measurement but can hardly be overestimated: the reduc-tion of empty spaces and the advance of the frontier (which took greater proportions after the eleventh century) must have multiplied many times the arable surface. The yield, in spite of technological advances which we shall consider later, nowhere came close to the proportions we would regard as adequate today: a crop amounting to about four times the seed seems to have been the average expecta-tion throughout the later Middle Ages, though fairly sharp varia-tions can be observed according to soil, years, and type of cereal. But the difference between a three-to-fourfold yield and the dismal one and a half or twofold yield of the Carolingian period divides a probability of survival from a probability of starvation. One failing harvest was enough not only to destroy the surplus of a normal Carolingian harvest, but also to deplete the seed stored for the fol-lowing year, especially as lords had to be fed and churches claimed their share, no matter how poor the crop. A fourfold norm, on the contrary, reduced considerably both the immediate and the long run consequences of one bad year.

Nevertheless, the margin between input of seed and output of crop remained too small to encourage bold experiments in quickening the cycles of cultivation. As an English manual of husbandry still warned in the late thirteenth century, it was better to make a good harvest every other year than two poor harvests every three years. This is probably the main reason why efforts at changing from a two-course to a three-course rotation, which were first recorded in the ninth century and made slow progress in the age of agricultural growth, were circumscribed to a few areas where the climate and soil were especially favorable and the yield could be sustained by a generous supply of fertilizer. Very likely the overall increase of production owing to such localized accelerations of the cycle of cultivation was smaller than the increase resulting from the modest, but more widespread rise of the average yield; and it would be premature to suggest at this early time a sharp separation between "progressive" countries with the faster cycle and "stagnant" countries with the slower rotation. Indeed, in all probability the greatest factor of increased cereal production was the expansion of the area under cultivation, and the most important novelty of the post-Carolingian period was the final elimination of seminomadic agriculture. This, in turn, by completing the ring of sedentary peoples brought to the farmers another dividend: the end of barbarian invasions, if not that of barbarous wars.

It is now time to turn from bread (and porridge) to *companaticum*. This will also help us to understand the shifts in the balance on which the whole system of cultivation rested. We have seen that the gap between a Mediterranean agriculture based on tight settlement with a prevalently vegetarian diet, and a continental agriculture resting on spaced settlement with a larger consumption of meat, had diminished during the early Middle Ages, but had not disappeared. It was further narrowed down in the age of agricultural growth; yet in some respects it became more visible. Horticulture, a great source of vitamins and one of the strongpoints of Roman farming, had been further developed by the Muslims in Spain and Sicily. In the age of agricultural growth Iberian and Italian farmers brought it to new heights under the stimulus of urban demand. They also paid special attention to beans, peas, and other leguminous plants, both as food crops and as fertilizers. As a matter of fact these plants get their nitrogen directly from the air, not from the soil. If buried they return nitrogen to the ground ("green manuring," recommended by Roman manuals and then again in an Italian manual of the thirteenth century); if eaten they are a good source of protein for men or beasts. Thus they can partly make up for deficiencies of manure and of meat in countries that cannot spare much land for cattle. Italy had experimented with all kinds of crop rotation in antiquity and continued to do so in the Middle Ages. Recent studies have disclosed a great variety of cycles, including three-course rotations. Apparently every farmer strove to obtain crops as often as his land would bear; in some cases, more than once a year. The danger was overcropping; for fallowing was always desirable, if only to restore moisture to the soil, and irrigation alone might be inadequate to offset the dryness of the climate. About Mediterranean France and the Iberian peninsula we know rather little: irrigation was widely practiced, but the two-course rotation seems to have prevailed.

A more regular alternation of winter sowing and spring sowing, conducive to the three-course system, was possible in the damper climate and heavier soil of northern France, England, and Germany. Though English manuals of the thirteenth century warmly recommend the accelerated cycle, documents do not indicate that its adoption was anywhere generalized. But it is in England and, still more, in France that we come across the earliest, most consistent examples of what was to become the standard rotation in the agricultural revolution of the eighteenth century: first year, winter wheat or rye; second year, spring grains and leguminous plants; third year, fallow. This proportion was often maintained even where fallowing was practiced in each field every other year (that is, when a threefold staggering had to be grafted on a two-course alternation of crops and rest). One is led to think that the basic reason was not a desire to accelerate the cycle but an attempt at playing safe with the whims of seasons. Spring crops were both a means to provide additional fodder and an insurance against a possible failure of a usually larger crop sown the preceding winter. No doubt northern Europe had larger and better pastures than southern Europe, but it also relied more heavily on meat and dairy; it could not fall back for *companaticum* on its meager supply of green vegetables, fresh fruits, or olive fats. If winter crops succeeded, spring fodder served mainly to fatten the herd and increase the stock of draught animals; if they failed, men could slaughter more animals and eat or use for seed the product of the spring crops.

It would be tedious to pursue one by one the other components of *companaticum*. Let us close with another reminder of the enormous difference between the diet of the rich and that of the poor. Most of the meat and most of the finer vegetables and fruit were normally earmarked for the table of the lord or the affluent farmer. There were exceptions when the coming of winter or a bad fodder crop rushed the slaughtering beyond the considerable capacity of the rich to consume meat or to salt it away, and when a bumper crop or a bad turn of climate threatened to spoil the vegetables. Hunting and an occasional catch of fish (sometimes, even of a stray whale) might offer extraordinary treats, but free hunting and fishing was more and more contained by seignorial preserves as settlement became tighter. It was hardly advisable to hang for a hare, and tame rabbits, the only medieval addition to domestic animals, were not as tasty as warren rabbits. Spices and other imported delicacies were totally beyond reach for the lower income brackets, until the thirteenth century at least. Only pork was fairly easily available to all peasants: a pig can feed on any scraps, and no lord would defy the immemorial custom of allowing at least one pig per tenant to share acorns with his own herd. Deservedly, the medieval pictorial and sculptural representations of the "labors of the months" always devoted three or four of their panels to the short career of the animal that brought joy to most people. Wine making also was good for a panel or two, but beer making did not seem worthy of special notice and was subsumed in the panels concerning the production of cereals.

ANIMALS AND TOOLS

Except where a different climate and soil called for another type of husbandry, medieval agriculture could not radically improve upon the best methods of classic agronomy. These were the fruit of a culture that had produced masterpieces in almost every field; even the most accomplished gentleman farmer of the eleventh or twelfth century would hardly know much that his Greek or Roman counterpart had not known better than he. Classic agriculture, however, was not overly concerned with saving human labor. This is the aspect of farming where the Middle Ages made their most significant contribution, not so much because scientific knowledge increased or because masters became more charitable as because the supply of labor diminished. A larger use of improved agricultural tools and animal breeds enabled fewer men to cultivate the same area as before and to expand widely into new land, including some that would have been unusable without the new technology.

When, where, and how widely were individual innovations adopted? The answer cannot be simple. The archaeological and written testimony is scant; worse still, it is often deceptive. The first mention of an important but unglamorous contrivance may be centuries later than its appearance; more centuries may elapse before the contrivance is widely adopted in a dynamic environment, and then again before it wins general acceptance or before its applications are worked out and put to use. In spite of improved communications, there still are surprising lags today: a wooden hook, first represented in Pharaonic art, still serves as a plough in Egypt; American restaurants have not yet realized the practical advantages of the espresso machine.

A shortage of labor first became evident in the late Roman Empire, but it was difficult to break traditions that had long been successful. The shortage continued in the barbarian age, but innovation cannot flourish in a weak, lull, incommunicative society. By the tenth century, tradition had been forgotten, inertia had been shattered, and the shortage had become less crippling. In post-Carolingian Europe slave labor was largely a thing of the past; serf labor, which now made up the bulk of manpower, was not increasing so fast that it could be ruthlessly exploited or thoughtlessly squandered. Necessity, the mother of invention, had found at last a congenial breeding ground. This does not mean, of course, that all medieval innovations were born at the same time. Some of them were a carry-over of Roman or Hellenistic contrivances that had not seemed very useful in the labor-rich classic world. A few originated with one or another of the barbarian nations, which by living in a different climate at a different cultural level had found useful solutions of their own; but it is often hard to decide which ones were already in use in the outlying provinces of the Roman Empire, or came in at the same time as the Barbarians, or were learned at a later time from Slavs and other peoples of the outer fringe.

Let us begin with a Hellenistic invention that made most of its progress in the Middle Ages: the water mill. It was used in antiquity for grinding cereals, but the high cost of installation and maintenance restricted its diffusion; rich men put their slaves to the grind, and the poorer housewives did their own grinding by hand. Only in the larger cities and exceptionally large estates would the cost of a water mill be covered by a steady, plentiful supply of grist. An Irish poetical legend credits a king of the third century with fetching "beyond the sea" a mill builder in order to give a rest to the slave girl who was bearing his child; but poets are not the best economic analysts. What caused water mills to multiply during the Middle Ages was a combination of two factors: slaves all but disappeared, and lords forced all of their dependents to send their grist to the seignorial mill. One third of the estates listed in a Carolingian inventory of St. Germain-des-Prés had water mills, some of them installed by the living abbot. By 1086 a good proportion of some five thousand mills that have been counted in England utilized the water of her innumerable rivers. Water power thus became the second major natural source of energy harnessed for human use; the first one, fire, had been captured as early as the stone age. The mill itself, gradually fitted for a variety of industrial uses was to become almost as ubiquitous in the later Middle Ages as steam, electric, or internal combustion engines in modern times.

In agriculture the competition of the water mill forced lords and farmers who had no running water or whose rivers were somebody else's property to replace millhands with animals; but animals, too, were badly needed for other farm work. A better solution was eventually provided through the windmill. A windmill is less powerful than a water mill and does not lend itself to diversified industrial applications; but it can be built almost anywhere at a moderate cost, and the wind is nobody's private property. All this explains why its origin and early diffusion cannot be followed as easily as those of the water mill. We do not hear of it in antiquity, but by the early twelfth century it is found in places as far apart as Iran and England, and its features vary rather sharply from one country to another. The most likely guess is that it originated at some time in the early Middle Ages in an arid, windy region of the Muslim world or of the Christian south (whether Byzantine or Catholic) and spread rapidly after the tenth century. But the last word on the problem has not yet been said. Windmills of different types may have been independently invented at different places.

The origin and diffusion of the heavy plough, which was better suited than the Mediterranean *aratrum* to the heavier soils of continental Europe, are still harder to trace. It certainly was not a Roman product, but we cannot decide whether it must be credited to the Gauls, the Germans, the Slavs, or some Central Asiatic nation; and perhaps each of these peoples was responsible for one of the gradually improved types that appeared in succession. The Roman *aratrum* was a fairly light, inexpensive, wheelless instrument of wood, usually strengthened with strips of iron, and fitted with a share that did not cut deeply into the ground. Conceived for the needs of dry farming, it enabled the farmer to cross-plough his field with at most a pair of oxen or asses, and even without a team if he could not afford one or chose to till almost inaccessible scraps of land; but it required much additional toil with spade and hoe. In spite of this shortcoming, low cost and easy handling insured its adoption throughout the Roman Empire. In France and England, for instance, it still was widely used at the end of the Middle Ages. Nevertheless a more powerful instrument, capable of cutting deep furrows, was desirable to tap the fertility of the moist, thick soils that abounded in continental Europe, and indispensable to open land that was literally inpenetrable to the light plough. It also would save most of the spade work.

The solution came through the insertion of wheels between the ploughshare and the team. The wheels served as a fulcrum for the ploughman to put more pressure on the share, supported larger and heavier shares, and lent mobility to an otherwise cumbersome engine. We catch a first glimpse of the heavy plough in an obscure passage of the Elder Pliny (first century A.D.), which mentions a wheeled *plaumaratum* (or *ploum aratrum?*—the word may have been misread by copyists), pulled by eight oxen, and used by some of the Gauls—probably those of the Po valley, Pliny's home land. If this instrument was the same as the *carruca* ("cart" in Latin, from which *charrue,* "plough" in French) mentioned in Carolingian documents, we can surmise a development like that of the water mill: a useful but costly innovation of antiquity made headway when labor became critically short and great landowners commanded the ploughing. But the story was probably less simple, because wheeled ploughs came of many types and at different times. Almost invariably one gets the impression that the first experiments were made on the Eurasian steppe and carried westward by migrating Barbarians.

We may omit a description of other improvements in the design of the plough and of virtually all agricultural implements—such details, important though they were, would be lost on any reader who does not happen to be conversant with medieval farming—but we must point out some of the repercussions in other fields. Nearly all of the improved tools called for a larger use of iron or steel. Though the Barbarians had learned in Central Asia highly advanced techniques for making, with inlaid steel, swords and buckles that were stronger and more supple than the Roman ones, they did not waste those laborious methods on ordinary farm tools. Carolingian inventories mention an extremely limited amount of iron and steel utensils, most of them intended for lumbering and carpentry; in the barbarian age a smith was not an ordinary artisan, but almost the equal of a goldsmith. Advances in farming equipment were interdependent with the multiplication of forges in the following centuries. The fact that smiths were for a long time more numerous in Italy than in the northern countries should make us cautious in estimating the speed with which the more efficient tools gained wide acceptance in the regions of Europe that needed them most. It also adds weight to the assumption that technical progress usually entailed a greater dependence of individual farmers on the powerful men or the organized village communities that alone could afford expensive equipment. To this we shall return later.

There was still closer interdependence between the development of tools and progress in animal husbandry and transportation. The heavier the plough, the larger the team. From this angle the northern countries, and the Barbarians in general, had a substantial head-start over the Mediterranean countries and peoples: they had larger pastures and larger herds. Oxen continued for a long time to be the preferred draught animals: they had more strength than donkeys, more patience than mules, more resistance to disease than horses, and they cost three or four times less in fodder than horses. Nevertheless in southern Europe one or two donkeys often were all a farmer could afford (and in Morocco one can still see today odd teams composed of a camel and an ass). In central and northern Europe donkeys were sometimes used, but it was no problem to get together a large team of oxen, and in the twelfth century oxen began slowly to be displaced by horses. All of these changes were connected with innovations in harnessing, feeding, and breeding, and we can no more decide where the first spark came than solve the problem of priority between the hen and the egg.

The Romans used to harness draught animals side by side. This was efficient enough when only a pair of oxen or horses was teamed, but it must have taken a skilled charioteer and a lot of space to get

The Old and New Attachment

SOURCE: "Classical" draft harness, eleventh century; illumination from Latin MS 8318 in the Bibliothèque Nationale. "Modern" draft harness, first half of tenth century, from an illumination in Latin MS 8085, Bibliothèque Nationale. Both as reprinted in Robert S. Lopez, *The Birth of Europe* (London: J. M. Dent & Sons, Ltd., 1966; New York: M. Evans & Co., Inc., 1967), p. 133.

good results from eight horses frontally harnessed for a circus race, and one wonders what would have happened with eight oxen frontally yoked to a plough. Tandem harnessing provided the obvious solution. Again, to keep the yoke in its right position on the withers of oxen the Romans used satisfactorily a simple strap around the neck. A similar device around the neck of horses, whose anatomy is different, interfered with their breathing. A stiff collar resting on the shoulders of the horse eliminated the difficulty. The hoof of the horse was not sufficiently protected by the "sandal" used by the Romans; the nailed horseshoe gave it fuller protection. All of these innovations probably came to Europe from different parts of Asia, much on the same tracks as heavy ploughs. Collar and shoe helped the horse to become a serious competitor of the ox; what could be done to help the latter? In Italy, oxen were sometimes shod; in France and Spain, their yoke was raised from the neck to the horns; the advantages, if any, were not significant enough for other countries to follow suit.

Medieval and modern partisans of the horse tend to link its progress from the twelfth century on to a drive for greater efficiency: its speed, they say, was more valuable than the stolid strength of the ox, especially in countries where rain and cold limit the good days for ploughing. But actually the contest was settled along national lines: France converted to horses (and in some cases to mules), Italy remained faithful to oxen (one pair was enough for her light plough), England often used mixed teams where horses had to adjust to the pace of oxen. Granted that medieval farmers were not as learned as modern agronomists, they must have used in their choice of draught animals some of the discernment they displayed in their experiments with new tools. In the early Middle Ages common sense forbad the use of horses except for transporting people: a good horse cost more than a slave. From the tenth century on prices fell down as careful breeding and generous feeding produced cheaper and stronger work horses (not without some loss of speediness); but there were other priorities to be taken into account. How convenient was it to raise oats for horses where one might have grown wheat for men? Would oats be a more suitable crop than beans in a cycle of production? Was horse manure a more valuable by-product than cow dung or, for that matter, sheep or pigeon droppings? Answers to these and other questions varied from place to place. Again we are thrown back to those problems of ecological balance which medieval men endeavored to learn by trial and error, and modern scientists strive to teach with moderate success—for now, as in the Middle Ages, food production has to make room for other economic activities; long range interests are at odds with immediate profits; and sheer stupidity takes a large toll of natural resources.

COMMUNITIES AND INDIVIDUALS

Whatever his personal inclinations, economic necessity made man a social being. The empty spaces of early medieval Europe offered to a few rugged individualists only a temporary chance to live dangerously alone. Sooner or later ascetics ran out of hermitages, frontiers got crowded, and isolated farms were enmeshed in villages. Living in a closely integrated community, on the other hand, extended to most individuals a better chance of survival when sheer survival was threatened, and a greater opportunity for advancement when things began to look up. Political circumstances worked the same way. Full liberty and independence were hard to shoulder for all but the most powerful people, and even these depended for power on the assistance of armed retainers and hard-working serfs. The barbarian age had seen first the decadence of the central government, then the failure of the Carolingian effort to restore it; the following centuries saw the growth of local government by powerful people (more specifically, of feudalism)—and, slightly later, the rise of town government in competition with feudal lords. Although towns, too, were communities, they broadened prospects for individual liberty wherever they could reach; but feudalism was by far the prevailing influence in the larger part of the European countryside between the tenth century and the twelfth, and continued to play a great role for the rest of the Middle Ages.

Feudalism is a system of government, not a form of agricultural exploitation; but two of its characteristics had a direct bearing on the organization of agrarian communities and must be mentioned at the start. On the one hand, it strengthened the hand of many landowners by giving them governmental powers and keeping the agents of the central government off their land. On the other hand, it tightened the solidarity of the community by upholding the notion that people do not "own" but merely "hold" God's land as a temporary trust, and that nobody, whether master or servant, can claim a right over another man without accepting a responsibility towards him. Lest this may lead us unduly to idealize social relations in the feudal age, let us add at once that in practice most lords shirked their responsibility while enforcing ruthlessly their twofold political and economic rights. Still the economic interdependence of all members of a community was a hard fact, not merely a political theory. In the limited horizon of a village the serfs and the lord (or, more often, the steward of an absentee or wandering lord) were bound together by a coarse familiarity, which was not unlike that of masters and slaves in the old American South, but probably less arbitrary because medieval serfs had better ways to hold back their cooperation or sneak out of the manor.

Manor (with its derivative, "manorialism") is the term by which English historians designate the integrated, self-centered, almost introvert village community that was prevalent in the larger part of feudal Europe. Like mansus (peasant homestead) and mansion (lordly house), manor comes from Latin *manere*, to dwell or to inhabit. This neutral, but chronologically circumscribed expression seems preferable to "economic feudalism," which refers to only one characteristic of manorialism, its congeniality with political feudalism. As a matter of fact what made a manor peculiar was not only the lord's power over it but also the tightly cooperative organization of an agriculture which had been designed to insure collective survival at the expense of individual initiative and of contacts with the outside world. Such an organization played in the hands of the lords, but predated him; it was enhanced by the introduction of new methods and tools requiring joint effort, but sank deeply into the grooves of barbarian and even prehistorical country life. In the primeval village nearly every activity had to be geared to the production of food and other elementary necessities; a modest surplus might be set aside for future emergencies and the support of religious and military leaders, but none could be shipped to still non-existent cities.

No doubt the medieval manor had gone a long way beyond that stage: the administrative superstructure had grown into the two classes of "those who fight" and "those who pray," proverbially contrasted with the lowly mass of "those who work"; production for the market was an indispensable if marginal part of the agricultural effort. Nevertheless the original postulates of earlier times were still in evidence: solidarity and team work came first, and cash payments did not make exchanges in kind obsolete. What gradually dissolved manorialism was not the decline of feudalism (for there could be manorial communities of free peasants without a lord, and feudal retainers living on cash fees rather than on land fiefs) but the growth of an extrovert economy based on the market. The more a manor contributed to what we call the gross national product, the less it maintained its original character as a self-centered, self-sufficient economic unit.

We no longer believe that there was a specific age to be called "the rise of money economy" or "the break-up of the manor." Money economy never plunged below the European horizon, and individual manors kept breaking up, that is, opening windows to the outside world. Yet for a long time and in a large part of Europe the inward pull of communities huddling for self-preservation was stronger than the outward push of individuals venturing out for self-fulfillment, with the sole exception of a few strong men. The age of agricultural revival gradually upset the balance, but the scale was tipped only where and when the revival of towns and trade threw a much heavier weight into it. Again and again, while the early expansion of European agriculture opens loopholes for peasants to seek more liberty on new land, we watch free men "recommending" themselves as serfs to a baron or to an abbot and free villages inviting a lord to be their suzerain, apparently without open constraint, because liberty without security is not yet a sufficient gift. This may happen at any time between the tenth century and the fourteenth, although instances become rare after the beginning of the twelfth and there are countries where by the ninth century the manor has lost its grip, if it ever had any. Hence, without ever forgetting that diversity is the essence of agricultural history, we still feel justified in referring to the first two hundred years after the turn of the demographic tide as an age of predominantly manorial, or self-centered, agriculture in the larger part of Europe.

It is much harder to choose a definition that will fit all kinds of manors. Probably the most convenient is still the one which was derived from a few English estates that first attracted the attention of economic historians: a manor is a village community where unfree peasants cultivate a lord's *demesne* or domain (land directly managed by him) in return for the use of another portion of his estate, while a substantial part of the land remains more or less open to all parties for grazing, gathering wood, and possibly trapping and hunting. Let us hasten to stress, however, that by the mid-thirteenth century, even in the most "manorialized" parts of England the definition fits snugly no more than one half of the villages. Some manors had no *demesne*, some had no peasant holdings, some had no unfree tenants, a few had not even a lord. If one crosses the Channel or merely wanders into Wales, the definition needs further stretching. Yet if what was once regarded as the "typical" manor is rather an extreme example or an ideal model, it brings out best the peculiar set-up that makes so many medieval villages different from modern villages and from the "typical" villages of the Greco-Roman world.

The division of the cultivated land into two parts, lord's *demesne* and peasant holdings, may have been a medieval trend if not an outright innovation. It resembles the political division of feudal kingdoms into several duchies or counties, one or two of which are a domain governed directly by the king with the help of his hired agents, whereas the others are entrusted to autonomous vassals in return for specific services. Since communications were difficult, and only a combination of land and status could buy the loyalty of the vassals, it was unpractical for the king to keep all of his territory in his hands, but dangerous to leave it all in care of others. The count of one county faced smaller obstacles with reduced means, and tried to meet them in a similar way. Whatever his rank and the number of manors under his economic control, the lord of a manor faced almost the same problems. Though the "villeins" who worked the land were much lowlier than noble vassals, they were not slaves; it was virtually impossible to deprive them of the house and plot they regarded as their own, except by offering them a secure place in the lord's household. Still the lord could not safely turn over to them all of the land and depend on their good will; nor could he easily keep in hand the whole manor, even if he delegated the task to his agents. The best compromise for him was to retain only a portion of the tilled land (usually smaller than the sum of the peasant holdings) and to maintain in his immediate service, beside the indispensable stewards and butlers, a skeleton team of farm laborers who would insure continuity of care. The other peasants, normally free to attend to their holdings, paid various dues in kind or in cash, and took turns in helping the resident staff of the *demesne* on a certain number of days in the week or year. Both dues and services varied from one manor to another, and in each manor according to status; for there were innumerable shades of serfdom, to say nothing of free peasants. Common pastures, waste and woodland also played a significant role in the economy of the manor. Lord and peasants shared them according to certain rules: usually, for instance, only the lord could cut trees, but villeins took dead wood for their hearths and green wood for their tools. The lord claimed a lion's share of hunting and fishing, if only for the fun of it, but the peasants clung stubbornly to their residual rights.

It is not surprising that there was endless bickering about the amount and nature of peasant dues, the sharing of common land, the responsibility for royal and religious taxation, and other details that made or broke the affluence of the lord and the welfare of the villeins. The struggle was not quite as uneven as it might look at first. The lord was the most powerful member and principal manager of the community, the chief judicial authority, and either God's representative (if an ecclesiastic individual or institution) or the representative's employer (if a layman). But the peasants had on their side their number, their passive resistance, their talent to erode and elude what they dared not oppose, and often their legal or illegal compacts. Above all, the entire community was aware of limits that could not be overstepped without wrecking the economic balance on which lord and peasants equally depended. This collective conscience expressed itself in the immemorial customs of the manor, suggested detailed regulations and timetables for work, and assigned to everyone his duties, his rights, and his land. The lord had to supply the temporal protection of the sword and the spiritual protection of the altar, the technical and legal experience of his agents, and the most costly permanent installations: mill, well, barns, often a repair shop. The peasants contributed, in addition to labor, their carts and the mobile agricultural tools. In his castle and his guarded preserve the lord did what he pleased; in their hovels and their vegetable gardens the peasants did what they could; in the open fields most agricultural operations had to be done in common, and innovations, if any, required general consent.

Even as the mark of the Roman chessboard is still visible in many parts of Mediterranean Europe and Africa, so the peculiar pattern of open fields has not been erased by later enclosures in a large part of Germany, England, and France, where it may have been established long before manorialism, possibly at the time of first agricultural settlement, or at least in the wake of a prehistoric invasion. Aerial photographs, which are excellent for bringing back the palimpsest of the earth, also show at some places, such as the Po valley, the encroachment of manorial agriculture on the Roman one: the rectangles where the contemporaries of Virgil hoed and ploughed in the privacy afforded by their hedges and stone walls underlay the strips where the contemporaries of Charlemagne carried out cooperative agriculture. As a matter of fact, neither the lord's portion nor

Survival of the Roman *Centuratio* in Italy

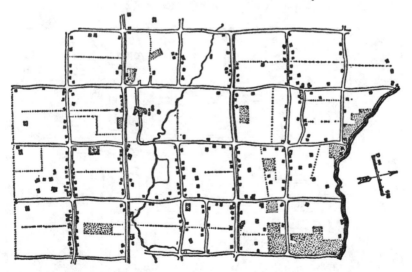

SOURCE: Checkerboard pattern of fields near Padua (after Meitzen). From *The Cambridge Economic History of Europe* (New York: Cambridge University Press, 1959); as reprinted in Lopez, *The Birth of Europe*, p. 54. Reprinted by permission of Cambridge University Press.

the peasant holdings formed compact blocks but usually consisted of a number of narrow slices scattered all over the manor. These ribbons of land were not separated from one another by permanent enclosures, but only by temporary fences. This arrangement apparently was dictated by practical reasons. The strips were open so that cattle could get in after the harvest, eat the stubble, and enrich the soil with manure. They were scattered so that each member of the community should have an equal share of good and inferior land, and partake of every crop raised on the manor—winter crop and spring crop, wheat and oats, beans, and, of course, grass where the soil had to rest. They were long and narrow so that the heavy plough should not have to turn too frequently; moreover, different farmers had to contribute beasts to the team, and none wished to work somebody else's land all day. This, at least, is the explanation scholars contrived, mainly in the nineteenth century, to make sense out of an allotment that looks strange to a modern observer. One could object that the heavy plough normally came later than the long strips, or

Typical Cultivation of a Medieval Manor

SOURCE: Plan of a village surrounded by open fields; the letters *a, b, c, d,* etc., indicate the owners having a strip in each of the fields. From Gordon East, *An Historical Geography of Europe* (London: Methuen & Co., Ltd., 1943); as reprinted in Lopez, *The Birth of Europe,* p. 176. Reprinted by permission of Methuen & Co., Ltd.

that the great difference in the number of strips held by individual peasants nullified whatever equality was provided by their being scattered. Nevertheless, the explanations are plausible, and it is difficult to test them since the peasants, who were the most interested party as they cultivated both their plots and those of the lord, are a silent race, and you cannot trust lords, stewards, or manorial judges to have always interpreted faithfully their thought.

We shall make no attempt at going over the multifarious variations and modifications of the manor in the different parts of Catholic Europe. Even a sketchy description would fill many pages without altering substantially the picture of the classic type. But we must note that the type lost many of its traits when and where feudal institutions were weak, towns were strong, law was written rather than customary, a large proportion of the peasants were freemen, and, above all, nature and tradition did not favor the open field and the heavy plough. All of these circumstances existed in some parts of southern France, of the Iberian peninsula, and more pronouncedly of Italy, ever since the beginning of the agricultural revival. That does not mean that all aspects of manorial economy were absent. Serfdom had made great strides in the early Middle Ages, the large estate under a powerful man was a familiar feature as early as the last centuries of the Roman Empire, common pastures and woods had pre-Roman origins. But one came easily across villages without a lord, lords without a demesne, and peasants cultivating their fields in severalty, that is, without reference to the community of which they were members. Although the growth of the population and the intensification of culture often caused excessive fragmentation of the land, efforts were continuously made to regroup the small plots into compact holdings; nor did the necessity of letting cattle in after harvest prevent farmers from building durable fences. Communal solidarity did exist, but it went mostly into special channels, such as collective care of the irrigation works, collective maintenance of roads, or collective resistance against the "unjust exactions" and "evil customs" that avid lords or their lessees tried to introduce.

Less progressive than northern France or England in certain sectors of agricultural technology, Italy was ahead of them in feeling the impulse of the Commercial Revolution. We cannot shift, however, our attention from self-centered to commercialized agriculture until we have examined the first, seminal changes on the front of trade.

3

The Take-Off of the Commercial Revolution

THE USES OF AGRICULTURAL SURPLUS

Even as demographic growth was a prime motor of agricultural progress, so agricultural progress was an essential prerequisite of the Commercial Revolution. So long as the peasants were barely able to insure their own subsistance and that of their lords, all other activities had to be minimal. When food surpluses increased, it became possible to release more people for governmental, religious, and cultural pursuits. Towns re-emerged from their protracted depression. Merchants and craftsmen were able to do more than providing a fistful of luxuries for the rich and a very few indispensable goods for the entire agrarian community. From this point of view, it is proper to say that the revolution took off from the manor.

It takes more than food surplus, however, to reorient a society from agrarian balance to commercial restlessness. We have seen that the Roman slave-exploiting landowners, who controlled the larger part of agricultural surplus, did not participate actively in business; commerce and industry expanded to a point, then settled down in golden mediocrity. The medieval lords on the whole were still more contemptuous of trade; the best one would expect of them was that they might patronize a slightly improved version of commercial and industrial mediocrity. A pattern of this kind may be observed in the long history of China, in spite of obvious differences in detail. China's ancient economy and society had many points in common with those of ancient Rome: agriculture was paramount, commerce and industry were adequate but marginal, security and stability rather than growth were the supreme ideal of the ruling classes. In the early Middle Ages demographic decadence and barbarian invasions upset the balance, but China had a prompter and fuller recovery than the European West. Frontier expansion was in full swing there while the Carolingians were still fumbling, early ripening rice swelled the crops while France was only beginning to convert to the three-course rotation, and the size and wealth of the Chinese cities dwarfed that of Marco Polo's Venice. In spite of this, China never had a commercial revolution; there was progress in size but no mutation in kind. Agriculture remained paramount, commerce and industry were still adequate but marginal, security and stability had been set on a higher level but still were the ideal of a basically unchanged society.

Halfway between the western and the far eastern world, a sharper change seemed in the making when the Islamic power emerged amid the depression of the early Middle Ages. The agrarian foundations of the society were shaken. Honest merchants, according to Mohammedan doctrine, deserved to sit in heaven with the martyrs and the prophets. Another writer pointed out that "the different peoples" of the earth had at long last been "brought together in mutual understanding." As a matter of fact, the early centuries of Islamic expansion opened large vistas to merchants and tradesmen. But they failed to bring to towns the freedom and power that was indispensable for their progress. Under the tightening grip of military and landed aristocracies the revolution that in the tenth century had been just around the corner lost momentum and failed. Without pursuing our comparisons any further, we may state that the European commercial revolution was a unique phenomenon, the unexpected result of a chain reaction that began almost accidentally in a few peripheral towns of Italy.

Let us consider again the notion of surplus. "A bare subsistence level" does not mean the same thing to all people, and is seldom identified with the minimum intake of food absolutely required to keep a man alive. Especially when the initial per capita consumption is not far above that minimum, a large proportion of food increases may be used merely to raise the level of subsistence. Unfortunately we cannot be too precise on that score. The elaborate attempts that have recently been made at computing in calories, on the basis of rare and dubious data, the improvements of the European diet during the Middle Ages inspire little confidence. Perhaps we can do better by the impressionistic device of comparing food served to the poor at different times and places: for instance, to the inmates of a Tuscan almshouse in 765, a measure of bread, two containers of wine, and two of a thick gruel of beans and millet drenched in olive oil or fat; but, to the inmates of a Champagne house in 1325, meat three times a week and either eggs or herring beside bread, oil, salt, and onions. The rich increased their food consumption much more, according to their status. All told, it would appear that rural northern France, southern England, and some parts of western Germany both grew and consumed the largest amount of food. They neither exported great quantities nor played a leading part in the Commercial Revolution; golden mediocrity was their achievement. Whether they gained in happiness what they missed in growth is not an economic but a psychological question.

There is some charm in the words ascribed to no less a man than King Louis VII of France (1137–1180), the first husband of Eleanor of Aquitaine and rival of King Henry II of England: "The King of England has men, horses, gold, silk, gems, fruit, wild beasts, and everything else. We in France have only our bread, our wine, and simple gaieties." Henry II was richer because his domains also included half of France but he fleeced his subjects and played havoc among his adversaries in order to win fame, extend his possessions, and crush ever-resurgent rebellions. Traditionally, the prowess of England's tax collectors matched that of the king. Louis VII was less warlike and cunning than Henry, and hence is known as an inept ruler. He might have spared his subjects, but for the fact that he was extremely pious and spent great sums on an unsuccessful crusade. In his time, the royal domain was small and France as a whole contributed little to the royal budget (the word, incidentally, derives from Old French *bougette*, little bag).

The king's vassals, both lay and ecclesiastic, took over where their suzerain stopped. Castles and churches mushroomed through the land and absorbed a considerable part of the available surplus of food and labor. A map of the simultaneous progress of vineyard planting and church building in the Bordeaux region illustrates the competition between spirits and spirit; far be it from us to extol the former above the latter, which produced inestimable moral and artistic riches, but the former had a stronger immediate impact on gross national product. And although castles cost less than cathedrals, and all wars by definition are defensive, the frequent crossings of armies that lived off the land and burned impartially all the huts and barns on their path consumed a good deal of resources. We do not need to pursue the impact of these and other incidental burdens on the economic growth of each country; nor can we calculate it with precision. The incidence, however, varied considerably and we have to keep it in mind when estimating the assets that were actually available for economic investment. No doubt church and castle building was not totally barren of profit (for the builders at least), and produced intangible dividends of material and moral satisfaction for the community. Even wars handed back to a few a fragment of what they took from the many. Still we cannot place on the same plane a primarily destructive activity and a constructive one, or expect the same results from a new bell tower as from a new water mill. Above all, medieval Europe had little room for investment over and above preservation of life. Granted that wars cost infinitely less than today, that the church rendered all sorts of educational and recreational services unobtainable elsewhere, and that government was far less demanding than the modern state, the sacrifice was proportionately heavier for the medieval man.

All this notwithstanding, enough surplus was left to give a commercial revolution a start. But who was there to make the first move? The claim that the very idea of craving for profit was alien to the feudal age is probably exaggerated: the acquisitive instinct is universal. Charlemagne displayed it in the management of his manors no less than in his wars of conquest. The abbots of Cluny were as proficient in collecting real and movable estates as in attracting devoted souls. With commerce, however, they were ill at ease; a man of high dignity might perhaps do some buying and selling through a trusted middleman, but would hesitate to expose his name on the market place. In the theoretical structure of feudal society there scarcely was room for a middle class between the exalted religious and lay lords and the lowly but irreplaceable laborers. Paupers were more acceptable than merchants: they would inherit the Kingdom of Heaven and help the almsgiving rich to earn entrance. Merchants were gold-hungry, said Rathier, the Belgian bishop of Verona; they were less useful than farmers who fed the entire population, said Aelfric, the English abbot of Eynsham; they did not know what honor means, said Ramon Muntaner, the Catalan soldier-adventurer. "Largess," that is, squandering wealth on gifts and conspicuous consumption, was one of the most honored virtues in Scandinavian sagas and Romance chivalry poems. Every code has its exceptions, but the bias existed in the tenth century as in the age of Augustus, in Germany as in China; it has not been entirely dispelled today. It took exceptional men in exceptional circumstances to break the spell and make commerce the most rapidly expanding, if not the largest frontier of the medieval West.

THE JEWS

The early medieval beginnings had been far from auspicious. What was left of local trade was in the hands of unimpressive native merchants (*negotiatores*), but long distance Mediterranean trade, the only one that offered substantial profits if not social status, was practically controlled by Easterners: Syrians, Jews, and Greeks. The Arab invasions did not end all relations between East and West, but opened to Syrian merchants wider Asiatic markets toward which they turned. Neither the Lombard nor the Carolingian conquests entirely wiped out Byzantium's shrinking footholds in Italy, but Greek merchants were encouraged by their government to wait for customers at home. Thus the Jews alone were left to provide a link, however tenuous, between Catholic Europe and the more advanced countries beyond it: the Islamic world, the Byzantine Empire, even India and China. At the same time, that is, between the ninth century and the eleventh, the Jews strengthened their position virtually in every locality of Europe where they saw a chance for trade. They dealt in salt, wine, grain, cloth, slaves, anything that any landlocked, countrified place had to sell or buy. For certain villages, the resident or transient Jew represented the only window open on the world.

The tenth century and the early eleventh marked the high point of Jewish prominence in long distance trade, not only in Christian countries, but also in the larger part of the Muslim world. The absolute volume of their transactions was of course restricted by the limited opportunities of that age, but their share of the total was so considerable that Frankish and Byzantine regulations of foreign trade often referred to "the Jews and the other merchants," as if Gentiles were a nondescript minority. The pronouncements of western rabbis on commercial matters and the correspondence of Jewish merchants in Egypt present the same picture of a wide and tight network of interconnected communities, whose members were keenly aware of what was going on in far-away countries and whose business methods were far in advance of those of their non-Jewish contemporaries, and in some respect even better than those of ancient Greece and Rome. Money lending was one of their activities, but it did not yet play a central role.

The peculiar economic position of the Jews was to some extent a by-product of their religious identity and social structure. There could be no idle military aristocracy among underprivileged aliens. Ecclesiastic pursuits could not become a full-time occupation, for even rabbis were expected to study the holy texts and explain them for the love of God, but to earn their living in an ordinary profession: Rashi of Troyes, the great eleventh-century scholar, was a wine merchant. Agriculture, the main occupation of the non-Jewish majority, was not entirely forbidden to the Jews, but the possibility of sudden expulsion and the difficulty of obtaining help from Gentile hands made it unattractive. Hence the Jews felt driven to concentrate their efforts and their money on trade. Literacy, an asset for the conduct of business, was fostered as a necessary tool for religious learning. Communication with foreign coreligionists, another asset, was an indispensable antidote to isolation within alien surroundings. It is true that some of the Jewish ritual obligations and interdictions hampered economic activities, but a most elaborate casuistry usually found ways to get around most difficulties.

On the other hand, although anti-Semitism did not reach its more virulent stage before the Crusades, the fact remained that the Jews were not fully accepted in Muslim society, still less in the Christian one. They were, at best, tolerated, but nowhere secure. This dark, dense cloud had a thin silver lining. Because the Jews were not full citizens of any state, they were nowhere full aliens; because they remained outside the religious community of the land, they were not required to observe all of its commandments. The function of neutral intermediaries between peoples separated by war or by different creeds, allegiances, and levels of culture suited them well. But they also were cast in a more unsavory role: that of a god-forsaken minority, singled out for malodorous yet lucrative tasks, which ranged from tanning hides to collecting taxes, and from ferrying slaves to extending loans at charges proportionate to high risks. Thus, partly by choice and partly by necessity, the Jews again and again emerged as pioneers and specialists in a great variety of important trades. Almost invariably, however, their very success increased their unpopularity. Sooner or later the moment came when needy princes or hungry mobs found pretexts to seize their property, kill or drive out some of them, and force the survivors to start again from scratch while their enemies dissipated the forfeited capital in immediate consumption or war.

So long as the Jews were allowed to retain their profits and to reinvest them more or less as they pleased, they quickened the economic development of every country where they lived. The Iberian peninsula; the regions between the Rhine and Meuse; and Provence, where they were especially numerous, drew considerable benefits from their presence. The city of Lübeck in her heyday bragged that she could do without Jews, but hardly any other town in central and eastern Europe could honestly make such a claim. In the long run, however, the luckiest Jews were not those who gained prominence among less enterprising Gentiles, but those who plied obscurely a marginal line of trade in one of the more dynamic countries where the native merchants did not depend on their help. Italy was the most notable example.

THE ITALIANS

There may be advantages in being less than a full citizen, but it is still better to be a citizen in more than one country. Multiple allegiance did not look peculiar or dishonorable in the feudal age, when almost every vassal owed loyalty to more than one suzerain and every land depended on more than one lord. Not only then, but at all times double allegiance was an inevitable remedy for a town or district that was caught between two warring adversaries and had to give some tokens of submission to both sides at once. This was the case of many Italian (more precisely, Italo-Byzantine) seaports that preserved their ties with the Byzantine Empire after their hinterland succumbed to either the Lombard or the Frankish conquest. Some of them had been prominent in antiquity, but the two seaports that emerged on top, Venice and Amalfi, had, remarkably enough, no Roman past. Their early history is shrouded in legend, but in both cases one extraordinary circumstance is clear much before the tenth century: the upper class owned some land but took an active part in maritime trade.

As early as 829 the will of Venetian Doge Justinian Partecipazio mentioned among his assets a substantial sum (1,200 silver pounds) invested in oversea commercial ventures. Venice was then practically independent, but honored her allegiance to Byzantium by supplying naval assistance, and used her eastern connections to unlock the gates of the Western Empire. She also maintained with Muslim Africa and the Levant as good relations as the sudden transitions from cold to hot war permitted. Thus she gradually built up a thriving triangular trade, based on the exchange of eastern luxury goods (mainly spices, silks, and ivories) and western heavy commodities (iron, timber, naval stores, and slaves). Moreover, the Venetians had two important wares of their own: the salt of their lagoons, and the glass of their furnaces. By the tenth century some glass blowers had made their way into the upper class, which thus acquired still another unusual component, master craftsmen. A writer of Pavia, the Italian administrative capital at the center of the Po valley, stresses the weirdness of the Venetian way of life:

"These people do not plough, sow, or gather vintage . . . They come with their merchandise and buy grain and wine in every market place." In the early years of the eleventh century the Venetians imposed their protectorate on a number of seaports of the upper Adriatic, but made no attempt at building a territorial empire that would have diverted their interests from sea trade to agriculture.

Amalfi looks like a variation on the same theme. Its autonomy began approximately at the same time as that of Venice; its prosperity also was based on the exchange of western and eastern commodities, to which local crafts added textiles of an unusually large size. There were, however, significant differences. Perhaps because her small territory was not safely encircled by lagoons but imperfectly sheltered by mountains, Amalfi had greater difficulty in asserting her independence from the lords of the hinterland, and failed to eliminate the competition of Naples, Gaeta, Salerno, and other seaports in her vicinity; eventually, in 1073, she had to bow to the conquering Normans, as did her neighbors and rivals. Again, maritime interests were less overwhelmingly prevalent than in Venice: Amalfi exported not sea-salt but olive oil, and her ruling class included many landowners. Lastly, whereas the Muslim side was the weakest in the triangular trade of Venice, Amalfi was strong in Constantinople but found her best rewards in Egypt. Not without dangers, however: in 996 rumors of an impending Byzantine attack and an accidental fire in the arsenal of Old Cairo aroused the mob against all Christians in town. We are told that more than a hundred merchants from Amalfi were massacred, that their lodgings were ransacked, and that financial losses amounted to about 90,000 dinars (84 pounds of coined gold), a staggering figure for the time. Even in the Byzantine Empire the Italo-Byzantine merchants aroused antagonism because they were foreign and because they enriched themselves; but unlike the Jews they were backed by governments and fleets of their own. They demanded, and obtained, special quarters where they could live according to their laws and beliefs, in relative security, with facilities for sleeping, warehousing, praying, and washing up. In the course of the eleventh century the continuous growth of their trade in the Levant and Africa was accompanied and fostered by the slower development of a network of extraterritorial enclaves or colonies, whose importance hinged not on the tiny surface they covered but on the rebates of tariffs granted to them and on the opportunities offered by the surrounding region.

As the progress of Venice and Amalfi was shifting the center of economic and naval power from the Byzantine and Muslim to the Catholic shore of the Mediterranean, two seaports from the "barbarian" part of Italy joined the race. Pisa and Genoa, too, were driven into a predominantly commercial way of life by an original handicap. In the tenth century their territory had been frequently laid waste by Muslim raiders looking for slaves and other booty; not even the towns had been spared. Led by their urban nobility, the Pisans and the Genoese fought back, expelled the Muslims from Corsica and Sardinia, and followed them up in their Spanish and African bases of operation. As the struggle went on, the economic structure of the towns changed: they built up their shipping, captured booty, and invested it in additional shipping with which they could trade. The turn of the tide was completed in 1088, when a combined fleet of Pisans, Genoese, and Amalfitans sacked "Africa" (Mahdiya, then the capital of what is today Tunisia) and withdrew only after obtaining commercial privileges. Six years earlier, a treaty between Venice and Emperor Alexius Comnenus had marked a similar turn: the Byzantine Empire, pressed simultaneously by the Turks in the east and the Normans in the west, bought massive naval assistance from the Venetians at the heavy price of exempting them from all the duties still paid by his own subjects in a whole row of Mediterranean seaports. The Mahdiya expedition, blessed by Pope Victor III and carried out by a Christian coalition against the Infidels, was like a miniature rehearsal of the First Crusade (preached in 1095); only the feudal host was missing. The treaty between Venice and Alexius Comnenus, which made the native Byzantine merchants underprivileged in their own land, was a distant premonition of the fall of Constantinople to the Venetians and the barons in the Fourth Crusade.

To all this we shall return later, but let us first pause a moment for an anecdote. Back in 829, when Venice was little more than a village and her Doge staked his money in commercial ventures, Emperor Theophilus began his splendid rule in Constantinople, then the largest and wealthiest city in the Christian world. One day, as he looked at the sea from the Great Palace, he noticed a beautiful merchant ship entering the port. When told that it belonged to his wife he angrily berated her—"God made me an emperor, you would make me a ship captain!"—and ordered the ship and the cargo to be burned down. A learned man, he certainly remembered the Roman law, taken over in a later Byzantine code, which forbad gentlemen to trade "so that the plebeians and merchants may more easily transact their affairs." (The law did not forbid the sovereign, however, to take a share of mercantile profits; traditionally the Greek ship owners were taxed so heavily that they could hardly increase their working capital.) Century after century, the Byzantine historians related with high praise the "act of justice" of Emperor Theophilus. The last to do so was a secretary of Alexius Comnenus, the emperor who had to mortgage the commercial future of Byzantium to Venetian ship owners. He did not see any connection between the justice of Theophilus and the injustice of Alexius; we do. Although in 1082 Constantinople still was the largest and wealthiest city in the Christian world, she was no match for her former vassal state where nobody was business-shy.

Still the rise of a few dynamic seaports would have had no revolutionary effect if the hinterland had failed to respond. Ancient Athens had created a commercial empire and fairly successful industries, but Greece as a whole lagged behind. Much more recently, Singapore and Hong Kong were islands of modern enterprise with a sluggish background. Tenth-century Italy, however, was ready—more ready than in the heyday of the Roman Empire. No doubt her towns had become smaller and poorer, but they had broken loose from the agrarian moorings that had held them back in antiquity. Most of them were ruled by a bishop or other lord who had no control over the district. The great landowners had deserted them for their castles or manor houses; there still was a fairly large number of minor noblemen who owned land in the vicinity and lived in town, but their weight no longer offset that of the majority of people engaged in trade and the crafts. Virtually all of the inhabitants were freemen and took some part, be it very small, in the municipal assemblies and the lower administrative tasks. Merchants as early as 750 served in the army on equal footing with landowners of equivalent income, and all citizens were responsible for the defense of the walls. These unique political and social circumstances enabled the Italian towns to react to the stimulus of demographic growth and agrarian revival more promptly than did the rest of Europe. As early as the tenth century, the opposition between those who fight or pray and those who work was not as significant as the solidarity of townsmen versus men of the country. The business fever, when it came, left almost no one untouched.

Perhaps the most telling change occurred among those noble families that grew too large to live comfortably off their inherited land. Outside Italy the supernumerary children tried to escape poverty and boredom through an ecclesiastic career, marriage to a noble heiress, or military service at somebody's hire. In the Italian towns they more often found the same opportunities and thrills by pooling their capital in business ventures, which involved a chance to pick up along the way a fight with pirates, brigands, unfriendly lords, and possibly Infidels. In turn, commoners who made good in their trade found no bars to political activity: the two leading families which vied for control over Rome while the popes and the emperors were locked in the Investiture Struggle (the Pierleoni and the Frangipane) descended respectively from a Jewish moneylender and a Gentile craftsman. Indeed it is usually difficult, in the scanty documents of the tenth and eleventh centuries, to tell apart the merchants who had bought real estate with the profits of trade, and were called "honorable" or "noble," from the noblemen who had sold their estate, invested the proceeds in trade, and married merchants' daughters. By the twelfth century all of them were lumped together as "magnates" (literally, "big shots"), while the rest of the people were known as "populars." The distinction, however, was based on wealth more than on status and did not prevent a much closer economic and political collaboration than that between noblemen and serfs in the manors and in many towns outside Italy. It was, hence, comparatively easy for the entire urban population to overthrow or buy off the town's immediate lord and establish a communal government of their own, under the direction of the magnates but with a measure of participation by all citizens. Because commercial and industrial activities were the main interest of nearly all members of the community, including the leaders, the states that thus emerged ("communes") geared their internal and foreign policy to the protection and promotion of business above all.

Local self-government was only a first target: it freed the citizens from the uncongenial administration of a lord whose interests could hardly coincide with theirs but made no room for expansion beyond the narrow territory inside and around the town walls. Like the agrarian revival, the urban surge was fueled by continuous demographic growth, which both drove the people to look for new outlets and made the new outlets springboards for accelerated demographic growth. It was a faster chain reaction than that of agriculture because a successful town attracted immigrants from the country; moreover, life expectancy seems to have been normally higher, probably because townspeople had a better diet and were less affected by local famines. It has been estimated (with a large margin of possible error) that the total population of England rose from 1,100,000 inhabitants in 1086 to 3,700,000 in 1346; but the population of Milan and Venice must have risen in the same period from less than 20,000 to well above 100,000 each.

Again, lords and peasants for a long period could gain space by clearing spare land of the manor; townspeople ever since the beginning needed more than spare building space within their reach. They wanted control over agricultural resources that would insure them against starvation, unrestricted access to outside sources of manpower for their enterprises, clear highways and low tariffs wherever their goods had to be routed, and open doors in as many foreign markets as possible. They also wished to complete their autonomy by eliminating all claims by higher suzerains to their money, their services, and their allegiance. It was obviously impossible for all towns to achieve all of these aims fully; one might almost say that the sky was the limit, and, besides, every town had to compete with others for most of the goals. Nevertheless, Italian towns as a whole made great progress on all fronts, not only by economic and diplomatic pressure, but also by resorting to open warfare to an extent that was unparalleled in the other parts of Europe where towns were growing and striving for the same aims. And though these wars diverted from economic production a good deal of resources, it cannot be denied that they yielded considerable economic dividends to the conquering communes.

We cannot linger on the intricate details of political and military history, but the outstanding, early success of the Commercial Revolution in Italy hinged partly on that of the bourgeois armies and navies that backed persuasion and entrepreneurship with physical power. It was not overly difficult for the major Italian seaports to gain mastery of the Mediterranean against the declining Muslim and Byzantine fleets, and to use their sea power as a bargaining instrument to get what they wanted from territorial lords who needed maritime support. During the Crusades and on other occasions requiring a crossing, Venice, Genoa, and Pisa assisted dukes, kings, and emperors not as subordinate towns but as fully independent states; only the seaports of southern Italy and Sicily eventually had to submit to the Norman kings and declined ever after. It was much harder for the towns of the interior to blast their way amid lords whose heavy cavalry was initially more than a match for the massed arbalesters and pikemen of the bourgeoisie. Still persistence and numbers gradually prevailed. Each town harassed the feudal rulers of its district, debauched their serfs by offering employment and protection, eroded the land around their castles, and finally forced them to become members of the commune as the only alternative to total ruin. Lastly, a league of Lombard towns defeated at Legnano in 1176 the supreme lord of Italy— Emperor Frederick Barbarossa—and won complete independence except for an empty acknowledgment of his theoretical suzerainty. Soon after, the Tuscan towns attained the same status without having to fight another battle.

This did not bring peace to Italy; there was continuous conflict between one town and another, and between powerful families and classes within each town. Conflict, however, was not peculiar to the urban world; the feudal world beyond the Alps, which on the whole managed to dominate the country and keep a hold on the partially self-governing towns, was far from peaceful. With an admixture of horror and admiration, a German chronicler who was a bishop and a relative of Barbarossa described northern and central Italy as a cluster of urban republics which obeyed no lord and put into highest public office "workers in the mechanical arts, who in other nations would be rejected like the plague." Obviously he overstressed the radical character of the new states: "mechanical workers," that is, artisans, still played only a minor role where money was the main source of power. In the twelfth century the Italian communes were essentially governments of the merchants, by the merchants, for the merchants—the ideal platform for the Commercial Revolution.

COINS AND CREDIT

Money, as represented in documents and physically preserved in coin collections, is the most available and possibly the most sensitive instrument to feel the economic pulse of the Commercial Revolution in its early stages. As usual, we lack overall figures, but the general outline is clear. Throughout Catholic Europe, but more sharply in Italy, the long deflationary trend of the early Middle Ages was reversed, approximately with the same timing as the population trend. The first tokens of change probably go back to the late Lombard period (eighth century) in Italy and to a somewhat later moment in other parts of the Carolingian Empire, but the real turn occurred in the tenth century. While payments in kind became increasingly rare, the mass of coinage grew at a much faster rate. It also changed in nature. Gold, especially useful for the largest payments or for hoarding, was no longer struck. Silver, useful for ordinary transactions and, when heavily alloyed with copper and issued in small denomination, for the smallest ones, not only reappeared where it had been abandoned as a monetary metal but became everywhere the only precious minting material. Pure silver, however, did not endure; coins were more and more debased by a growing proportion of copper, and their weight also was diminished. By the end of the twelfth century each of the Italian communes issued nothing but miserable looking, brownish, tiny deniers whose silver content was but a small fraction of the silver denier of Charlemagne. When the Italian merchants wished to pay large sums in cash without carrying heaps of their puny coins they had to use a variety of foreign coins, ranging from the English silver penny (which, almost alone in Catholic Europe, had not been debased) to Byzantine and Muslim gold coins; or else they could use ingots of precious metals, or, again, nonperishable spices and other commodities as valuable as precious metals.

What do these developments suggest in terms of economic growth? Since coins are struck at the order of governments, the simplest answer would be that kings, dukes, and communes spent more than they could afford and tried to cover their sins by imposing the same face value on less and less good metal. To a large extent this is true, but in the long run—and, in a commercialized society, even without delay—no government can nullify the laws of economy, whether it knows them or not. People have a way of realizing that money is no longer what it used to be—more easily so when it consists of hard coins that can be weighed, assayed, and told by their color—and respond to debasement by raising prices. Higher prices force the government to strike a larger amount of money unless price control is established. The last man who tried to stabilize prices was Charlemagne, and he failed. Another explanation that has been offered is likewise inadequate though not factually inaccurate. The rapid increase of goods and services available for money made it impossible for the mints to turn out as many good coins as were needed. Some precious metal was obtained by melting works of goldsmithry, a larger amount by stepping up the exploitation of mines, and an unknowable quantity by importing it from the Byzantine and Muslim world through war action and a favorable balance of trade, yet the supply never caught up with the demand. This, too, is probably true, but if the mass of money had been chronically insufficient one would expect prices to decline, in terms of precious metal if not in face value of coins. We know on the contrary that real prices, with a few exceptions, went up. It has been calculated that the cost of living in England quadrupled between 1150 and 1325. Hence we must conclude that the velocity of circulation also increased.

This was a consequence rather than a cause of the general acceleration of exchanges, but governments unwittingly contributed to the process. The more they debased the coinage, the faster the coins changed hands in daily payments for humbler goods and services that had previously been hard to get on a retail basis. The baker sold individual loaves to consumers who had been wont to make their own, to have it made by unpaid dependents, or to purchase it intermittently in large quantities for storage; the mason worked for daily wages and took care of small jobs for occasional customers instead of committing himself to a single employer in return for food and lodgings. Large amounts of debased coins, foreign coins of higher value, or ingots served for substantial transactions when hard cash was absolutely required. A growing proportion of business affairs, however, was carried out more conveniently by credit operations, and these further multiplied the velocity of circulation.

Unstinting credit was the great lubricant of the Commercial Revolution. It was altogether a novel phenomenon. We have seen that the Greco-Roman economy was well supplied with cash of all kinds but ill-suited for commercial credit on a large scale, and that the economy of the barbarian age was deficient both in cash and in credit; it never got far off the ground. The take-off of the following period was fueled not by a massive input of cash, but by a closer collaboration of people using credit. It did not occur in Germany, where new silver mines began their activity between the tenth and the twelfth century, but in Italy, where the gulf between agrarian capitalists and merchants was narrowed down. A few members of the lower nobility dehoarded precious metals, a few moneyers transformed bullion into coin, a few sailors and soldiers got hold of war booty. These modest contributions to the existing capital went a long way because credit enabled a small investment of hard cash to go to work simultaneously at more than one place.

This development has to be surmised rather than proved on the basis of scant indications in the sources of the tenth and eleventh centuries; its consequences become clear by the twelfth century, when the movement of capital can be followed in the more abundant documentation of a few key cities. No doubt we still find a good number of straight loans at high interest rates, most of which look like usurious consumption credit rather than commercial investments; but a larger proportion of the contracts explore novel formulas of partnership and other arrangements for the sharing of risks and profits. To this the Church may well have contributed by its insistence that loans are sinful unless they are "gratis et amore Dei," that is, granted without interest in the spirit of charity; but it would be a mistake to ascribe solely to religious influence a change that stems from the same cooperative attitude involved in the collaboration of men of all classes in the political struggle that lead eventually to the emergence of independent communes.

CONTRACTS

The development of commercial contracts is as crucial in the history of trade as that of tools and techniques in the history of agriculture. Only a few contracts are clearly related to Greco-Roman ones. The others are almost certainly medieval innovations, but the accidental staggering of the extant documents, and the tendency of commercial practices to spread rapidly along trade routes, make it hard to decide when and where a new type of contract first occurred. As we proceed from Byzantine hagiographies of the seventh century to Arab legal texts of the eighth, Jewish commercial correspondence of the early eleventh, scattered Venetian contracts of a slightly later period, and ultimately a mass of Genoese notarial records of the twelfth century, chronological data must be rearranged according to logical deductions, and no conclusion can be safe until, in the thirteenth century, the same basic contracts seem to be available throughout the Mediterranean world.

Still it is significant that the contract which displayed the closest cooperation among fellow merchants, though first mentioned in Muslim law and occasionally found in the earliest Venetian sources under the name of *rogadia* ("by prayer"), seems to be especially popular with the African Jews, whose togetherness was strengthened by the special dangers of minority status. Under the stated terms of *rogadia* a merchant pledged to transport goods of another, and presumably to trade with them, as a friendly gesture and without compensation. If the contract did not conceal a charge that was unmentioned in order to escape religious sanctions against "usury" (for interest taking was forbidden among fellow Jews as well as among Muslims and Christians), we have to assume that merchants took turns in lending free assistance to one another, even if they were not joined in a partnership. This patriarchal contract, however, soon became obsolete in Venice and seems to have been unknown in other western towns. It was later replaced by the contract of *commission,* whereby a merchant took care of another's business for a percentage commission or a fixed fee; but this became convenient only when and where the risks of trade diminished.

A better rewarded but more committing solidarity was created by partnership (*societas*), a Greco-Roman contract which survived in medieval law. Partners pooled their capital and labor and shared both profits and risks. Unfortunately every partner was held jointly and unlimitedly liable for the debts of the others: that is, a merchant who intended to invest a small sum for a short time could lose everything he owned if any of his partners incurred obligations they were unable to honor. The danger was smaller in partnerships for the operation of a petty craftsman's workshop or a retail store, which neither required nor attracted much capital and credit, but was a serious threat in trade on a larger scale. In the latter case it seemed preferable to graft the conventional bond of partnership on a more reliable tie, the family. The earliest documents of Venice bear witness to the popularity of the *fraterna,* not so much a partnership of the Roman type as an adaptation to commerce of a patriarchal institution: the joint administration of goods inherited by two or more brothers and invested in trade. By the twelfth century a more flexible contract, the *compagnia* (from *cumpanis* or companion, "sharer of the same bread"), offered a better solution. It brought together not only brothers but also less close relatives—mostly cousins, but also sons-in-law chosen among the brightest employees—and required only the investment of a limited sum for a limited time. Liability, however, still was joint and unlimited for all partners.

Ordinary partnerships and family partnerships never lost their prominence in land trade. The former grew in numbers but not in size, for mediocrity was the price of safety: the unsatisfied creditor of a small shopkeeper might not even suspect that the debtor had partners. The *compagnia,* on the contrary, tended to expand in a large number of inland cities ranging from Piacenza and Asti to Lucca and Siena. The partners extended both their family and their investments; they renewed the contract after the first term had elapsed, and often welcomed outsiders' contributions "above the social capital," that is, interest-bearing deposits resembling modern bonds. Success, however, usually led to overconfidence: sooner or later one of the partners contracted a "bad debt," and his insolvency dragged the others into ruin. Nevertheless the trade and credit offered by the partnership while it lasted had promoted independent activities which were not necessarily involved in the failure. Up to the mid-thirteenth century no *compagnia* became large enough to wreck by its collapse the economy of a whole town. Even as business cycles did not prevent the long-run economic growth of the nineteenth century, so the boom-and-bust pattern of the medieval *compagnia* did not interrupt the main upward trend of land trade.

Maritime trade, on the other hand, neither needed nor could afford such a pattern. The *fraterna* soon become obsolete in Venice and probably never appeared in Genoa; the *compagnia* was represented mainly by detached agents of foreign partnerships whose home was in an inland city. Joint and unlimited liability was an intolerable hazard where the greatest prudence and honesty could not prevent total loss on account of shipwreck or piracy. Happily, no commitment had to exceed the duration of a one-way or, at most, a round-trip voyage, for every affair had its natural conclusion with the arrival (or failure to arrive) of the goods, after which new commitments could be undertaken on a clean slate. The solidarity of a family was less crucial than that of people in the same boat. As early as Greco-Roman times the latter had suggested agreements to apportion the contribution of merchandise each voyager would have to jettison if needed (the so-called Rhodian sea law); early Byzantine custom (the Nomos Nautikos) had added provisions in a similar spirit for the sharing of risks and profits. The contract of *column,* widely used in Amalfi and other Italo-Byzantine seaports of the south as well as in the Dalmatian town of Ragusa-Dubrovnik (but, apparently, not in Venice), probably stemmed from there. All contributions of capital and labor by those who traveled on a ship —captain, sailors, merchants—were listed in a column of the ship log; risks and profits were shared according to the value ascribed to each contribution. Thanks to its patriarchal character the contract has survived down to our days in the small fishing business of the Adriatic, but it did not suit capitalistic forms of trade. After the twelfth century, the *column* fades away from records.

Greco-Roman law made large use of another contract, the sea loan, which remained in favor throughout the Middle Ages although it gradually lost its prominence. Like the ordinary loan, it entailed an interest charge and did not involve the lender into a partnership relation with the borrower; but restitution of the loan, which was extended only for the duration of a single or round-trip oversea voyage, was waived in case of total loss on account of shipwreck or enemy attack. This clause enabled the parties to claim that the charge was not "usury" but what we would call an insurance premium. Sea loans are very frequently encountered in the records of every Christian seaport, but their popularity diminished in the mid-thirteenth century both because the popes ruled that the premium was in fact usury, and because insurance began slowly to develop as an independent form of business. Moreover, maritime trade like land trade called for closer collaboration than that of a straight loan. This need was met by another contract, the *collegantia* ("colleagueship") or *commenda* ("recommendation"), which joined the advantages of the sea loan (duration for a voyage only, no liability of the lender towards third parties) with the main advantages of the partnership (sharing of risks and profits between lender and borrower, no suspicion of "usury").

The *commenda,* which some modern writers improperly call "sleeping partnership," was a medieval innovation of the highest importance and contributed greatly to the faster growth of maritime trade as compared to the slower progress of capitalistic forms in land trade. Its place of origin is still debated: the Islamic and Byzantine countries seem to have the best claims, but the western *commenda* differs from its oriental counterparts in some details, and one cannot rule out the independent emergence of similar contracts at different places. In its simplest Italian forms, a stay-at-home party lent capital to a traveling party who was expected to invest it in commercial operations for the duration of a round-trip voyage. The lender bore all risks of capital and was entitled to a share of the profits (three-fourths in the majority of cases). The managing borrower bore all risks of labor and kept back the rest of the profits. Third parties came in touch with him alone and had no claim against the lender, whether or not they knew of his existence.

Inasmuch as the lender ostensibly received without personal effort the larger part of the profits (and in most of the earliest contracts gave specific instructions to the manager concerning the destination of the voyage and the type of wares to be bought), one would think at first of an unequal association of a rich capitalist with an impecunious laborer; but this was by no means the most frequent case. The same man could be simultaneously a lender in some contracts and a borrower in others; that is, he spread his risks and multiplied his profits by adding capital of his colleagues to such part of his own capital as he took along on a voyage, and by entrusting the rest of his capital to colleagues traveling to other seaports. Again, an impecunious man could take his chance in big business by entrusting a small sum to a great merchant who would not spurn the smallest contribution to his working capital. As for the unequal apportionment of profits, it probably was largely off-set by the fact that only the manager really knew how much profit had been gathered; in early contracts he was expected to back his accounting with some kind of proof, but at a later time the lender pledged to believe his word "without an oath or a witness." In conclusion, the *commenda* was the closest medieval antecedent of our joint-stock companies, which attract investments of any size from all kinds of people, are limitedly liable, and do not feel bound to give detailed accounts to stockholders. No doubt a *commenda* lasted only for one voyage, but nothing prevented a satisfied lender from entrusting his capital to the same manager again and again.

All the contracts we have mentioned, and others we have been forced to omit, involved credit; this tended to reduce the merchants' need for specialized credit institutions. What we could call banking developed slowly on three independent levels: pawnbrokers, deposit bankers, and merchant bankers belonged to different social classes and specialized in different types of credit, although they might dabble in one another's business as a side activity or move from their level to another. Jewish pawnbrokers in Italy were outclassed and outnumbered by "Lombards" (Christian natives of Chieri and other northwestern towns) in the unsavory but indispensable line of lending money against a pawn to the poor, improvident, or unsuccessful traders and to other people whose credit was not good. A pawnshop was entitled to the same grudging toleration as a house of prostitution: its owner was seldom molested but knew that he was heading for eternal damnation unless he repented and returned his "ill begotten" profits to the Church, stewardess of the poor. Interest charges were of course high but did not normally exceed those exacted today by small loan agencies, which face far smaller risks in this world and the other.

Deposit banking was a more honorable line, although in the strict definition of the Church it also would be classed as "usury." It was an almost spontaneous offshoot of money changing. During the day a changer displayed a heap of coins on his *banca* or bench in a public place; at night he locked it in a well-guarded coffer. It was easy for him to lend any surplus he might gather in the exchange business, and easy for others to use his coffer to deposit coins they did not immediately need. This led the changer to grant credit to reliable customers at a much lower interest charge than a pawnbroker, and to pay a still lower interest to people who allowed him to use money deposited with him. City governments asked him to keep an eye on circulation, denounce forgeries, and occasionally to advance cash to the treasury. They required the changer to keep a reserve that would cover his outstanding obligations, and in return recognized the entries in his book of accounting as legal proof of a disbursement. Gradually the practice prevailed for most merchants to keep an account with a banker and carry out their local transaction by a simple transfer on the banker's book, without any cash changing hands. In turn the changer granted credit, usually by allowing a customer to make an overdraft; but he had to beware of overextending his operations lest a rush on his funds exhaust his reserve and swallow all of his goods. Deposit banks grew more slowly than *compagnia* partnerships for trade; yet, almost invariably, they eventually were dragged into the same boom-and-bust pattern.

Large scale credit for long distance operations was part and parcel of contracts among merchants. It took longer to become an independent line of business, mainly through exchange contracts negotiated by the largest merchant companies. The process was well on its way by the late twelfth century, but it can best be described in a later period, when merchant banking fully matured.

TRANSPORTATION

By releasing agrarian income for investment in business and by making credit operations more flexible the Commercial Revolution had removed two of the main stumbling blocks that impeded economic growth in antiquity. It was less successful in eroding another block, inadequate mechanization. Unlike contracts and other mental techniques, which can be improved at little or no cost, tools require considerable investments for delayed rewards; there was progress, but no revolutionary change. We have already come across certain innovations in agricultural hardware, and in the next chapters we shall take up a larger number of novelties in industrial equipment. Transportation, which is as essential to commerce as currency, must be briefly considered here.

Land transport, even today more expensive than transportation by water, found its most serious limitations in the condition of roads. For all their shortcomings, the Roman ballasted highways were a considerable legacy to that part of Europe which had been welded together by the imperial might; but their upkeep would have required a strong central authority commanding huge gangs of slaves or drafted laborers. They slowly broke down through centuries of neglect, and whatever was left of long distance trade in the early Middle Ages had to depend almost entirely on internal waterways. Meanwhile a new, more flexible and complex, but flimsier road network began to take shape. Towns were linked to one another not by a single master highway, but by several winding trails of beaten earth and loose stones, sometimes bolstered by wooden planks. Each trail offered an alternative connection whenever war, unbearable tolls, or bad weather made another way impassable. Like most other aspects of public works and services, roads were now built and maintained mainly by private industry (half-commercial, half-religious organizations being at the forefront) at a minimum cost in money and labor. It is hard to tell whether the economy gained by diminished expenses more than it lost by increased impediments to heavy traffic. No doubt the diffusion of tandem attachment, the stiff horse collar, and the horseshoe, added power to animal traction; so did the introduction of axled pairs of cart wheels in the place of independent wheels which tended to lose their parallel alignment whenever a turn was made. (Independent wheels still make it hard to turn smoothly baby carriages and tea wagons, which normally have no axles.) But heavy carts cannot be used on nonballasted roads except on dry, even soil.

A high proportion of late medieval transport was more happily entrusted to pack animals, especially mules, which were more suited to rugged mountain crossings. Progress in this sector was tied not so much to better saddles and bundles as to improved breeding and feeding, which placed at the disposal of merchants cheaper and sturdier beasts, and secondarily to the horseshoe. Between the ninth century and the twelfth the price of mules dropped radically, and their numbers steeply increased. No longer was it necessary to heap crushing burdens on the shoulders of porters, forced by serfdom or need to carry loads over the highest hills. Muleteers and carters, however, did not thrive enough to form powerful companies; land transport remained the business of small entrepreneurs, petty craftsmen rather than capitalist merchants.

Transportation by sea opened broader perspectives. A small boat might cost no more than a pair of mules and carry a trifling load, but large ships were in the top class of capital goods—so much so that their construction, ownership, chartering, and operation gave occasion to credit arrangements, investment pools, and risk-and-profit sharing contracts as complex as those of commerce proper. Indeed long-distance traders, shipowners and ship captains in the larger maritime cities often belonged to the same social group and would easily swap or combine roles. Far from exploiting them as ruthlessly as the Roman and early Byzantine governments had done, western rulers of the later Middle Ages who needed the cooperation of shipowners dealt with them in the same gingerly, if not quite respectful, way that they treated people able to advance credit or supply military support. Their own governments would of course require naval service whenever necessary, but hardly ever without equitable compensation and usually for purposes directly relevant to the shipowners' welfare. Nor were owners and captains the sole beneficiaries of commerce carried out through their ships; sailors normally were entitled to take along some freight of their own and to add to their salary the profits of trade. The popular image of the galley slave fits both late antiquity and the early modern period but not the Middle Ages, when labor was scarce and oarsmen were proud, free citizens and tough fighters. Initially the change in status of ordinary sailors probably was one of the many effects of the demographic depression of the early Middle Ages. Their subsequent rise to higher income brackets, however, was due to the fact that the world of shipping was copiously irrigated with money.

Shipbuilding has a good deal in common with architecture; it called for almost as much skill, imagination, and daring as the construction of the great medieval cathedrals and castles. It would take too long to describe in detail the different types of ships and their component parts or tackles; let us only point out that the need to provide suitable vessels for a great variety of purposes and the desire to combine to a smaller or greater degree the advantages of sails with those of oars led to incessant and fruitful experimentation. Everything else being even, propulsion by oars insured a higher average speed and greater independence from changes of wind and weather, especially if the deck was long and narrow enough; but it required a large crew which swelled the payroll, consumed food, and competed with cargo for the available space. Propulsion by sails economized everything except time (and even time if the wind happened to be favorable), but made a ship more vulnerable to storms and enemy attacks, the latter a constant danger in the medieval circumstances; military protection could be sought for by the addition of soldiers to the sailors, but soldiers were just as costly and no better fighters than oarsmen. The most successful vessels were a compromise between oarship and sailship, the characteristics of the latter being more valuable when bulky and inexpensive cargoes were carried, and less acceptable when speed and security were essential for the transport of precious wares on dangerous waters.

Two basic traditions existed side by side and exercised some mutual influence: that of the northern seas, which was grafted on the prehistoric tradition of floating hollow tree trunks, and that of the Mediterranean, which had acquired far greater sophistication in Greco-Roman times and continued to evolve. In the early Middle Ages even the hollow tree trunk (*monoxylon,* as the Byzantines called it) rendered great services: cargoes were normally small, and the light Viking ships could easily be transferred to the smallest internal waterways and carried on men's shoulders on short waterless stretches. With the addition of planks joined at an angle to the trunk, which thus acquired the function of a keel, the northern ship could become more capacious. The more planks were added, however, the harder it became to balance the ship under sails. As for the full potential of the keel, it was not realized before the last two or three centuries of the Middle Ages, when northern Europe began to shorten the economic gap that separated her from the more advanced south.

The Commercial Revolution of Italy and the western Mediterranean put to work every kind of ship, from lithe, tiny rowboats to broad, roomy sailing "nefs," but tied its fortune especially to the galley and its many relatives. A repeatedly improved descendant of the standard Roman ship and of later Byzantine models, equipped almost equally well for oar and sail propulsion, for commerce and for battle, the galley fully justified her name, "swordfish" or "galeoid shark" (*galaia* or *galea* in Byzantine Greek). The wooden spear that prolonged her pointed bow was capable of breaking a hostile ship as easily as the elongated hull broke the waves; a complex system of masts and sails, including some triangular ("lateen") ones, enabled her to make the most of any wind, in spite of the handicap of a rather flattened keel. There were different varieties of the galley, and the dimensions could be altered according to cargo and speed requirements, but length was always emphasized against width. The larger the ship, the easier it became to bear the overhead of a numerous crew. As a matter of fact, sizes tended steadily to grow, but not nearly as much as the churches and fortresses built by contemporary architects. Although shipbuilders had to be more careful of economic considerations than cathedral builders, whose reward was in heaven, they coped with space problems by increasing the number rather than by expanding the size of ships. Cost problems were usually met by combining in each ship a sufficient amount of light, precious commodities with a sufficient bulk of heavy merchandise, which had the additional advantage of stabilizing the narrow vessel.

Venetian Galley of the Fifteenth Century

SOURCE: Bas-relief on the Contarini tomb, Padua; as reprinted in Lopez, *The Birth of Europe*, p. 139.

Let us not hasten to proclaim that medieval shipwrights lacked the skill or the courage that at a later period produced the great carracks, cogs, and caravels of the "age of discovery." Economic growth could proceed no faster than the expansion of production and consumption all over Europe. So long as it was difficult to fill large ships at one stroke by calling at a few main seaports, a galley had to remain small enough to enter a large number of minor harbors and often to anchor at open beaches. Short haul navigation was necessary not so much because of technological shortcomings—navigational instruments by the twelfth or early thirteenth centuries were almost as advanced as in the Renaissance—as because the lack of good inland and coastal roads made it imperative to unload cargoes as close as possible to their final destination. In turn, roads would not be improved so long as economic growth did not put sufficient pressure on people who were to use them; and since economic growth depended partly on good roads and large ships, transportation was enmeshed in a closed circle. To pry the circle open, the Commercial Revolution needed the collaboration of producers and consumers everywhere, the merchants providing the spark, the whole society offering the fuel. It was a long process, which we shall describe in the following chapters.

4

The Uneven Diffusion of Commercialization

THE NERVE CENTERS
OF THE REVOLUTION

An economic revolution is not as sharply defined as a political one. Both the Declaration of Independence and Adam Smith's *Wealth of Nations* are of 1776; but while no one will question that the American Revolution broke out in 1776 and attained its goal by 1783, it would be impossible to single out an initial and a terminal date for the Industrial Revolution and preposterous to expect that it could achieve radical change in less than ten years. The same can be said for the Commercial Revolution, a concept that has not yet won as general acceptance as that of the Industrial Revolution, mainly because a large number of economic historians have little training in pre-modern history and little inclination to look for radical change where the lack of reliable statistical material limits the opportunities for quantitative study.

Quantity, however, is only one dimension of history and does not provide clear-cut subdivisions within a millennium of sustained growth. With the exception of approximately two centuries (from the mid-fourteenth to the mid-sixteenth, but the interval was not exactly the same in every part of Europe), the economy of Europe has been expanding ever since the tenth century. Naturally the figures of our day dwarf those of the Industrial Revolution; these in turn are much larger than those of the Commercial Revolution. The chain

reaction of mutually strengthening factors, however, does not substantially differ from one subperiod to another. The population
increases; per capita production soars; technology progresses; means
of payment and transportation become faster; both capital and consumption respond to the contradictory but not incompatible stimuli
of concentration in the hands of a few leaders and distribution to
previously underprivileged people; underdeveloped regions get involved in the general movement; the whole economic process affects
more and more deeply the social structure, the shape of culture and
the entire way of life.

To define the Commercial Revolution as opposed to subsequent
phases of economic growth we must consider not so much the differences in quantity as the mutations in kind. Even as industrialization
gave the leading role to the industrialist, so commercialization transferred economic leadership from the landowner to the merchant.
This does not mean, however, that merchants became the richest,
most powerful, most numerous, or (least of all) most prestigious
class throughout Europe. In fact, at no time during the Commercial
Revolution did agriculture lose its place as the occupation or livelihood of the overwhelming majority; indeed, it still was predominant
over the wide expanses of Europe a good many years after the beginning of the Industrial Revolution. Yet commerce between the tenth
century and the fourteenth became the most dynamic sector of the
economy in one country after another, and merchants were the main
promoters of change. Like industrialization at a later time, commercialization did not spread evenly. We have singled out the Jews and
the Italians as early starters; let us add that throughout the Commercial Revolution no other group concentrated its efforts on trade
as thoroughly as the Jews and none entirely matched the drive of
the Italians. Some nations, however, eventually almost caught up
with the latter, whereas a few owed whatever progress they made
not to local initiative but to foreign merchants visiting their markets
or coming to their towns.

Towns were the nerve centers of the Commercial Revolution; no
wonder, for under any circumstance a concentrated population re-
sponds to economic stimuli more promptly than a scattered one.
Medieval urbanization and commercialization were mutually sup-
porting phenomena; but we must remember that town development

need not be linked to commerce more than to industry or agriculture. We have seen that the heart of the ancient city was the public square where landowners discussed politics and farming. Their substantial and diversified consumption, and that of the local administrative, military, and religious officials, supported a number of merchants and craftsmen, but did not make them equal partners. Many craftsmen were slaves; many merchants lacked citizen rights; and in many of the innumerable Roman "cities" agriculturists and officials were not only more influential and wealthy but also more numerous than the trading class. The Commercial Revolution did to the medieval city what the Industrial Revolution was to do to the entire European scene. It gradually shook the numeric, economic and political predominance of landowners and officials and made the market, instead of the public place or the cathedral squares, the main focus of urban life.

The term "market" (from the Latin *mercatum*) may mean both a gathering of merchants and their gathering place. In the latter sense, the Romans used more commonly the term *forum,* and they ordinarily called a merchant *negotiator,* that is, business man. During the later Middle Ages "market" and "merchant" (*mercator*) gradually crowded out the older words, probably because in the barbarian period the withering of urban life had made permanent market places and resident business men superfluous in all but a few towns. There was not enough to do for traders to get together every day at the same place or wait for customers in a shop. The collapse of continuous trade, however, stressed the significance of periodical gatherings, and these would grow in numbers, size, and complexity wherever and whenever economic activities picked up. They ranged from weekly or monthly encounters, where townspeople and country people of the immediate surroundings exchanged handfuls of local goods in the course of a few hours, to annual affairs, usually lasting several days, where customers from a larger area bought provisions for the whole year, sold any surplus they produced, and got hold of a few outlandish objects. At their lowest level, daily markets opened no more than a loophole in a wall of self-sufficiency: many transactions were carried out directly between the producer and the consumer, sometimes by barter, and nobody had to spend the night away from home. Annual markets, usually called fairs after the *feria* (feast or holiday) to which they were linked, called for more complex arrangements. Any empty space might do for professional merchants to set up their stalls and pitch their tents (*tienda* still designates the shop in modern Spanish), but they would not come from afar unless they had some assurance of free and easy access, some advantages and conveniences during their stay, and, of course, a reasonable chance for profit.

Urban growth did not destroy the temporary markets, which had been ordinarily confined outside the walls or segregated in the yards of churches and castles, but eventually transferred the bulk of trade to what we might call the shopping and business sections of the town. Stately halls for sectional or specialized trade, covered plazas and arcaded alleys, long rows of craftsmen's houses with a shop open on the street came alive in a picturesque disorder of which we can still get an idea when we visit the suks and bazaars of certain Muslim towns, from Marrakesh to Istanbul, where industrial pollution has not yet replaced preindustrial dirt. The more important transactions of wholesale or luxury trade were carried out more discreetly in the office of a notary or a guild, the inner rooms of a merchant's mansion, the private quarters of a sea captain or the premises of a company of merchant bankers. Obviously not all towns attained the same size and complexity, but many of them fitted the statement of Chrétien of Troyes, the famous French writer of the late twelfth century: "One might well believe that in a city a fair is being held every day." More proudly, a Florentine chronicler of the early fourteenth century pointed out that his city had no use for special markets or fairs: you could buy and sell any amount of anything at any time. He exaggerated but slightly: Florence at her medieval peak, with a busy population of better than 100,000 inhabitants, a mint output of 500,000 gold florins a year, a wool production of 80,000 pieces of cloth, a meat consumption of 4,000 oxen, 80,000 lambs and 30,000 pigs, a wine consumption of 25 million quarts, a fertile district ruled by her independent commune, and the largest business companies in the Christian world, hardly needed the stimulus of periodical marts.

In all but a very few urban centers, however, markets and fairs continued to play an important role. Some economic activities are essentially seasonal: the gathering of certain crops, the opening of snow and icebound routes, the sailing dates for large convoys of ships, the traditional time for shearing sheep, preparing cheese, or delivering cloth to the wholesaler determined spurts that could best be channeled into a fair. Travel took a long time, and a merchant would be encouraged to take a specific trip if he knew that he would reach an extraordinarily large number of his colleagues and an unusual variety of goods. Moreover, markets and fairs tied their fortune to special facilities and privileges not normally available on the spot. Not many towns outside northern and central Italy enjoyed full independence and still fewer controlled the country around them; ordinary trade, therefore, had to cope with all kinds of obstacles in the unfriendly context of a feudal government and an agrarian society. No doubt the interests of lords and farmers were not in everything different from those of towns and traders, nor was unrestricted commercial liberty the ideal of most towns. A compromise was always possible, but it would be more easily attained for the limited duration of a fair than for the entire year. Lords and towns alike would then be willing to interrupt any war, lower any toll and tax, waive the customary restrictions on the residence and activities of aliens, grant speedy and informal justice according to international commercial law, strike abundant coinage of good and uniform quality, recognize and enforce written or verbal obligations, renounce such obnoxious customs as *aubaine* (confiscation of the property of deceased aliens), *ius naufragii* (seizure of the goods, and sometimes of the survivors, of wrecked ships), and reprisal (forfeiture of the wares of all fellow citizens of a defaulting merchant). Even the greediest prince and the most protectionistic town usually realized that at least temporary concessions were needed to get a market going, and that a going market would bring money and supplies outlasting the suspension of normal burdens.

Still if the absolute volume of transactions in markets and fairs kept increasing as the Commercial Revolution progressed, their share of total trade inevitably diminished. Seasonal factors cannot be entirely eliminated, but a steadier demand will elicit a more evenly distributed offer; sailors and muleteers will prolong their operations under all but the most forbidding weather; and craftsmen will use stocks of raw material to spread their work throughout the year. By the late thirteenth century a Pisan manual of business foresees only one slack month out of twelve, and the detailed notarial records of Genoa show no serious variation at any time of the year. Less successful cities on peripheral shores or in the countrified center of Europe are more sensitive to seasonal fluctuations, but a city that for a long series of years has attracted peasants to her weekly market and merchants to her annual fair will normally become a permanent nerve center of trade.

As early as the seventh century the "Lendit" fair near Paris may have been the prime factor of the commercial ascendancy of the city, but by the thirteenth century its concentrated activity added no more than a trimming to the continuous trade of a hundred Parisian guilds. As for the Champagne "fairs," which eclipsed all others from the late twelfth century to the early fourteenth, they owed their success to the fact that they had less and less in common with the traditional annual marts. Held at four towns of the same region, in an unbroken rotation that encompassed practically the entire year, they served mainly as money and commodity exchanges for merchants who converged there from all parts of Europe and were hardly interested in local affairs. Commodities were represented by samples, if at all; cash was almost entirely replaced by instruments of credit; the location of Champagne, astride some of the main roads from the Mediterranean to the North Sea and from the Channel to the Baltic, supplied a suitable common ground for business by correspondence and payments by compensation of credits and debts. But when the Italians, who had been the most important patrons, began using their ships to go directly to the North Sea coast and established permanent offices in Flanders, the Champagne fairs withered away.

Apart from seasonal and intermittent flurries, the special "liberties" connected with markets and fairs had insured their early success. This prop, however, did not last long; for as merchants gained power and self-assurance, they demanded and obtained the same liberties wherever and whenever they visited a town. Commerce thrives on freedom and runs away from constriction; normally the most prosperous cities were those that adopted the most liberal policies. No doubt military power and economic superiority often interfered successfully with free competition: thus the English kings continued to herd foreign purchasers of wool in appointed ports and "staple" centers, and the Venetian republic submitted German importers of spices to rigorous controls. Even in these cases, however, it is doubtful whether restrictions really improved the position of a nation that produced the best wool and of a city that had access to the best spices; with looser regulations, Spain sold large amounts of wool and Genoa gained a good share of the spice market. This, however, is not the place for a retrospective examination of the merits of protectionism and free trade; the available data for the Middle Ages are too incomplete to warrant general conclusions in a moot debate which even today is influenced by political as well as economic considerations.

PATTERNS AND OBJECTS
OF TRADE

Not the least contribution of urban to commercial growth was the insertion of the fresh, sustained, and widespread demand of a middle class between the relatively unelastic demands of two largely self-sufficient classes: a few landed rich who could afford but seldom needed to buy, and many landed poor, who needed to buy but seldom could afford it. Salt is indispensable for survival, and some people will not live without costly jewels; but the Commercial Revolution got its fuel mainly from the multiplication and diversification of both customers and wares. Its success was marked by the fact that, although the flow of merchandise and the volume of transactions increased faster than the total population, prices kept going up and governments worried more and more that supply might be outstripped by demand. No doubt per capita consumption rose at all levels as greater productivity and better distribution made higher standards of living possible for all classes; but nowhere was the rise as directly translated into commercial growth as in the towns, because townspeople produced specialized goods and depended on trade for nearly everything else. Against the concentrated temptation of desirable objects displayed in the shops and acquired by a next-door neighbor, the sermons of ecclesiastic or lay moralists and the frequently enacted sumptuary laws were of little avail. Inevitably, the luxury of yesterday tended to become the treat of today and the necessity of tomorrow.

We must not, however, overestimate a consumption drive that even in our days does not hit all people with the same intensity. Starvation and poverty have not yet disappeared in the United States, and the average living standard in a small Mississippi town is far below that of a northern megalopolis; the spread of prosperity in medieval Europe was much more uneven. Indeed, a rapid economic growth tends to increase the distance between minimum and maximum levels. At the highest level many kings and dukes in the thirteenth century were better off than Emperor Charlemagne in the ninth, but there were noblemen who still lived on the edge of poverty in isolated castles. The conspicuous consumption of the upper bourgeoisie in a large Italian or Flemish city matched that of the highest English or German nobility, but the middle class in the great majority of towns had to be content with little. At the lowest level, the diffusion of shirts may perhaps be taken as a test case for economic and social differences. Strictly speaking, a shirt is not a necessity; it does little to protect its wearer from the cold, but adds to his comfort and also to his health as it can be frequently washed. Virtually nobody in the early medieval West wore anything under his dress; the very word *camixia* ("shirt" in Latin) is of late medieval origin. But coarse hairshirts made their appearance toward the end of the barbarian period among the richer and sophisticated people. It took many centuries before Italian peasants generally wore them, still longer before they entered French farmhouses, and the Commercial Revolution did not introduce them everywhere else. Meanwhile the Italian bourgeoisie and the French nobility grew so accustomed to better underwear that they began to regard a hairshirt as an instrument of penance. French literary sources nevertheless insisted that lower class people ought not to pamper their rough skin with smooth underwear; German sources complained that they often did; only in the most developed regions of Italy was the wearing of linen or, at least, cotton shirts among farmers and petty workmen taken for granted.

These illustrative examples may be enough to indicate the lags between one country and another. One wishes there were precise figures to measure the lags quantitatively, but we must be content with a few approximations. It has been calculated that by the late thirteenth century the taxable exports from England (by no means one of the least developed countries in Europe) often amounted to a quarter million pounds sterling a year; but this, even if we consider that the English pound was worth at least four Genoese pounds, is much less than the almost four million pounds of taxable exports and imports that went through the harbor of Genoa in 1293. In turn, the Genoese figure seems to be roughly ten times as high as the value of exports by sea from Lübeck, the most important German port, in 1368. Again, Italy in the early fourteenth century had four cities that attained or surpassed 100,000 inhabitants (Venice, Milan, Florence and Genoa), but Paris apparently never reached that figure. Ghent (the largest city in highly developed Flanders) may have had 50,000 inhabitants, Lübeck and London were smaller, and many of the German "cities" had no more than one or two thousand inhabitants. No doubt the difference between Italy north of the Tiber and the most retarded parts of Europe during the Commercial Revolution was as significant as that between England or the United States and India or China during the Industrial Revolution. Such discrepancies forbid generalizations about the impact of both "revolutions." Any attempt at calculating an average between maximum and minimum growth (or no growth at all) would bring no meaningful results. The most convenient solution is to keep the underdeveloped majority in mind, but to focus attention on the economic leaders, if only because their activity is better documented.

At first glance, if we compare the patterns of trade in the Commercial Revolution to those in the Industrial Revolution, certain differences will strike us, apart from the already noted fact that all proportions are almost unbelievably smaller. Luxury products and the custom of the rich tend to play a more important role than commodities for mass consumption. Many if not all business men show greater interest in enlarging profit margins on a limited number of sales than in enlarging the number of sales on a limited profit margin. Even the strongest and most specialized partnerships seldom turn down as irrelevant or insignificant any business that comes their way. A fairly large part of retail exchanges do not require the intervention of a middleman, as many craftsmen sell some of their product in the front window of their own shops and many free peasants bring some of their produce to the daily or weekly market. All of these characteristics were the heritage of antiquity and of the early Middle Ages; development did not change old patterns overnight. Still the volume of exchanges will look impressive enough if we bear in mind that the sea trade of Genoa in 1293 was three times as large as the entire revenue of the kingdom of France in the same year, when King Philip the Fair encountered the greatest difficulties in raising that amount of money. Likewise, the other characteristics that in modern perspective would belittle the image of the Commercial Revolution change aspect when set against the background of their time.

What limited trade in ordinary and bulky goods was not so much the lack of a potential market as the high incidence of transportation costs on wares that had to be moderately priced. Hence most of it had to be carried out locally or regionally, on a small scale and with feeble concentration of capital. Such petty transactions left little trace in extant documents. This makes it hard for the economic historian to observe their increase during the Commercial Revolution, which may nevertheless have been proportionately greater than that of luxury trade. It has been estimated that by the early fourteenth century as much as 100,000 barrels of wine were exported from Gascony to England in a single year, mainly by small traders and on small ships. This particular figure may have to be revised downward, but there is no doubt that salt, grain, preserved fish, nonperishable fruit, cheese, timber, nonprecious metals, wool, cotton, and some ordinary dyestuffs were shipped in ever-larger amounts, at longer distances, and on bigger vessels as time went by. Waterways and roomy sailships (or barges, when a small river or artificial canal had to be utilized) were the preferred means of conveyance, but even the heaviest commodities might be loaded on a galley or another fast ship when they were urgently needed or in order to add weight to the light and valuable wares included in the cargo. Even transportation by land became more convenient as roads were improved all over Europe. Progress was especially important in the Alpine passes, which could best withstand the competition of waterways by offering shortcuts between the Mediterranean and the northern or northwestern regions. The opening of the St. Gotthard pass in 1237 with a new road and bridge for pack animals and the widening of the Septimer to fit small carts in 1338 were the most significant breakthroughs; they diverted towards Germany some of the traffic previously directed to Champagne via the western passes and in turn forced French transport agents to improve their services.

Land routes played a smaller role in northern Europe, but by enlarging their ships (usually at some sacrifice of speed) the merchants of the "northern Mediterranean" (North Sea and Baltic Sea) promoted a trade that depended heavily on basic raw materials and other bulky goods whose production entailed comparatively little labor, such as timber, cereals, and salted fish. The merchants of the classic Mediterranean had a much greater choice of refined commodities, but took advantage of the generally higher living standard and denser population to call at every port and pick up every crumb of possible trade. (This, incidentally, was the positive aspect of what is often disparagingly called their lack of specialization.) Venice, for instance, never relented in her efforts to increase her hold on the salt market, which had been her earliest trump card, and handled by sea, river, or land route large amounts of grain, oil, wine, iron, copper, tin, mercury, timber, fruit, soap, live animals and slaughtering meat, ordinary leather goods, and coarse textiles, in addition to the best luxury products that labor could make and money could buy.

It was, however, the latter that afforded the best chances for gain and produced and required the largest concentrations of capital. One thinks at once of spices, that prestigious class of wares which is usually associated with medieval long-distance trade and almost neutralizes the vulgar odor of herring and beer with an inviting aroma of cinnamon and nutmeg. What went under the general name of "spices" in the middle ages, however, was not all prestigious, aromatic, or expensive. The most detailed manual of commercial practice in the early fourteenth century, by Francesco di Balduccio Pegolotti, lists alphabetically no less than 288 items, almost evenly divided between "gross" and "minute," under the heading of spices. Besides a compact group of seasonings, perfumes, medicinals, and dyestuffs, we come across commodities as unrelated to one another as copper, cotton, wax, paper, and glue. Again, a large number of Pegolotti's "spices" come from the Muslim and Byzantine world or the farther regions of Asia and Africa, but many are products of Italy and other European countries. Not included or barely mentioned in the list, but more profusely described elsewhere in the book, are many other wares of any type, price, and origin, such as staple foodstuffs, furs (mostly from northern Europe), twenty-three varieties of raw silk (mostly from the Middle and Far East), and the vast, nearly ubiquitous family of textiles. Apart from the almost total omission of most manufactured goods of iron, wood, and glass, the manual accurately reflects the extreme variety of the objects of international trade at the zenith of the Commercial Revolution but does not help us to classify or rank them according to their importance.

Without trying to rearrange or complete this panorama, let us single out the leading components of the main axis of international trade, an axis that had Italy as its pivot and joined northwestern Europe with the Levant. Throughout the Commercial Revolution the strongest assets of the Levant fell into two groups of high priced raw materials: spices proper (that is, seasonings, medicinals, and dyestuffs), topped by pepper, which was almost as important as salt to add flavor and preserve food while refrigeration was unknown; and fineries ranging from precious stones and ivory to raw silk. Objects of industrial art also played an important role in the earlier years, but Italy gradually beat the Orient at its own game and turned from importer to exporter. Europe at first struck a balance mainly by exporting to the Levant nonprecious metals and timber in bulk, but soon added to the list a growing variety of industrial products: glassware, arms and other iron ware, and above all woolen and linen cloth. Imbalances one way or the other could be corrected by shipments of gold and silver, which might offer incidental profits if the ratio between the two metals was different at the two ends of the axis; but the stock of precious metals was quickly exhausted. The best solution normally was to make the aggregate value, bulk and weight of eastbound shipments as closely equivalent as possible to those of westbound shipments, so that the potential of means of transport might be fully exploited both ways and that the entire initial investment might work for profit from beginning to end.

How much profit? Obviously no generalized answer is possible. In the Middle Ages as now, the average rate of profit tended to be related to the average rate of risk, but individual stories ranged from triumph to failure. High risks and high profits were predominant in the early stage of the Commercial Revolution; they were instrumental in forming the first accumulations of capital and lifting a number of intelligent and fortunate merchants above the general mediocrity of early medieval traders. The Three successive *commenda* agreements of 1156–1158, whereby a Genoese investor trebled his initial investment of slightly more than 200 pounds, and the traveling party earned almost 150 pounds as his share of the profits, are a characteristic example of good fortune. Later, competition forced down the average profits, but greater security and the widening of the market enabled careful managers to increase their assets more steadily than ever before. Commerce then lost much of its adventurous and almost heroic features; it tended to become a routine, which the senior members of the merchant class could direct from their desk, through branch employees and commission agents, instead of accompanying personally a large proportion of cargoes. In Italy by the early fourteenth century the average interest rate on commercial loans had declined to between twelve and eight percent. (At the same period, in a fairly prosperous German town of the interior, Nuremberg, the legal rate was 43 percent, but the Holzschuher company charged 94 percent for loans to Jews!) Yet there always remained sectors and kinds of trade where war, piracy, storms, sharp fluctuations of demand and supply, great distances or unfamiliar surroundings offered to an adventurous man an opportunity to pursue high profits and risks. In 1341 the Venetian merchant Francesco Loredan carried to China a recommendation letter of his uncle, which said in part: "If this journey goes well, I shall live comfortably the rest of my days; if it does not, I shall sell all I own." Only a brief survey of the uneven progress of commerce and merchants in various directions of the compass can give us an idea of opportunities encountered and the way they were, or were not, seized.

THE MEDITERRANEAN SCENE

We no longer regard the Crusades as the main turning point of European economy from inertia to aggressivity and from poverty to riches. The turn came earlier, chiefly through internal changes: the growth of the population, the increase of agricultural production, the emergence of a self-confident merchant elite. Still it is undeniable that the great Christian offensive against Islam (and later, against the "bad Christians" of Byzantium) dramatically en-

Principal Mediterranean Seaports and Colonies

larged the surface of contact between the fast developing society of Catholic Europe and the riper but less flexible societies on its eastern and southern borders. Actually this kind of encounter had already occurred in two regions which were totally or partially reconquered from Islam in the eleventh century: Sicily and Spain. Both before and after their return to the Christian fold those regions enjoyed exceptional prosperity, less because of their own production than owing to international trade. "Come to Palermo for business and pleasure!" writes a Jewish merchant to his correspondents in Muslim Africa. Similar spurts occurred in the states of the Crusaders and later in various lands taken from the Byzantine Empire; the details belong to political, not economic, history. Yet neither Sicily nor Spain nor the Holy Land nor the Byzantine territories preserved any lead by the thirteenth century, when the center of gravity had definitively moved to the "big four" of northern and central Italy (Venice, Milan, Genoa, and Florence), whose powerful merchants had a firm grip on the routes towards the fertile and industrious European hinterland and endeavored to reach far beyond the declining Islamic façade into the depth of Asia and Africa.

The durable economic value of military expansion, which often produced backlashes in the slow withering of occupied areas and the exasperated hostility of unconquered countries at the back door, consisted chiefly in the customs rebates and physical facilities offered to merchants abroad. We have seen that concessions of this kind had already been granted to citizens of Venice and other Italian seaports in a small number of Byzantine and Muslim harbors. In the twelfth century the Crusaders were more generous, both because immunities or (as we would say today) extraterritorial rights fitted within the feudal pattern and because they obtained military and economic assistance in return: many Italian communes and a few seaports of southern France, Catalonia, and Dalmatia obtained fiscal privileges and autonomous quarters, encompassing in certain cases entire sections of towns and small suburban plots. By the end of the thirteenth century the Muslims had reconquered all of the Crusaders' holdings, but much wider opportunities had opened elsewhere. In 1204 the conquest of the larger part of the Byzantine Empire by "Frank" barons and

Venetian seamen had given the latter bridgeheads in every port and made Venice the sole ruler of Crete and other Greek islands: "one fourth and a half of the Empire," it was said at the time. In 1261 the Byzantine emperor assisted by the Genoese recovered Constantinople; still the Venetians kept most of their gains and the Genoese in turn built a similar colonial empire at the expense of their ally. On the other hand, repeated attempts by Frank armies and Italian fleets to conquer Egypt or parts of it failed. This, however, did not prevent the merchants of several Italian, southern French, and Catalan towns from obtaining customs rebates and physical facilities in a large number of Muslim harbors all along the African coast and what was left of Islamic Spain—not by force but by diplomatic means.

An admittedly rough evaluation of tolls collected by Genoa from traders using her facilities abroad clearly shows that political control was not as essential as free access to markets: in the fourteenth century the revenues from Pera, a suburb of Constantinople that formed a walled enclave under Genoese rule, were less than double the revenues from Alexandria, where Genoa merely rented a small cluster of buildings (*fondaco* or *fondoq*) which the Muslims locked up at night. In turn the revenues from that *fondaco* were more than one fourth as large as toll revenues from sea trade in Genoa herself. Nevertheless we should not minimize the effects of sea power and territorial expansion. Diplomatic pressure paid off not only because the policy of granting privileges to foreign merchants was as acceptable in the Byzantine and Muslim seaports as in the feudal markets and fairs of the West, but also because the presence and superiority of western naval forces all over the Mediterranean could not be safely ignored. The fact that most ships could be used interchangeably for commerce and for war made the interplay of economic and military power tighter. Again, territorial expansion tore down barriers that diplomacy could at most lower; the cost of occupation and defense might be high, but each of the Italian colonies had some agricultural or mineral resource and markets that could be profitably developed.

The combination of war and trade was equally effective in the mutual competition of European seaports. No doubt each town relied primarily upon the skill, capital, and organization of its merchants, the natural and artificial advantages of its harbor, and whatever local agricultural and industrial resources were at hand. An early start and the sophisticated business methods we described in the preceding chapter placed Venice in the lead; Genoa, the only sea town that succeeded in catching up with her, owed a good deal to her flexibility in the face of new and bold techniques; yet neither tradition nor innovation could remain forever the exclusive property of two towns. To maintain and increase their edge, both Venice and Genoa found it necessary to fight. Venice made good her claim to supremacy over the Adriatic by subjecting many seaports to her rule and forcing others to accept limitations on their long distance trade. Genoa found it harder to affirm her primacy over the broader expanse of the western Mediterranean, but she subdued the entire Ligurian coast, beat Pisa in a protracted struggle for control over Corsica and parts of Sardinia, nipped in the bud the expansion of Narbonne, Marseille, and Montpellier, and yielded as little ground as possible to Barcelona, a late comer which showed unusual ability to grow. Unlike the northern Italian seaports, which were independent communes, the French and Spanish seaports were somewhat handicapped by the overhanging power of a feudal lord or a king, who collected heavy tributes and often embroiled them in his own quarrels; Barcelona, however, had the good fortune that the king of Aragon, her overlord, almost always backed her. At any rate, if the winners at war reaped the best rewards of long distance trade, the losers found some compensation in the continuous expansion of short-haul navigation. Only Venice, Genoa, and to a smaller extent Barcelona were fully equipped to defy enemy fleets and pirates and sent large convoys of ships straight out to a network of far-away ports which obeyed or respected their flag. Satellite seaports could save overhead costs and risks by specializing in the redistribution of imports and exports along the coast.

Internal trade more often than not shared some of the characteristics of satellite sea trade. There were no long and untrammeled crossings under heavy military protection from home port to a colony or a privileged landing place, but a slower progress along routes of which only the first stretch was home territory and the others, if any, were subject to tolls and petty harassment by foreign governments. Only the communes of northern and central Italy ruled a considerable amount of territory and tried to enlarge it in a relentless struggle: Milan, Florence, and to a more limited degree smaller centers such as Verona and Lucca succeeded in subjecting other communes to restrictions like those imposed by Venice and Genoa on satellite ports. In the other Mediterranean countries the towns of the interior were lucky if they controlled the immediate suburban space or could rely on the protection of a strong territorial lord. These shortcomings, however, mattered little in markets and fairs; for those who attended them a series of bilateral agreements, multilateral alliances, and collective shows of force made long-distance journeys tolerably safe. Self-interest persuaded all powers along a route not to cut their own throat by imposing exorbitant tolls or letting robbers go unpunished, since dissatisfied merchants would make a detour through more hospitable land. When two cities on the Po River wanted to get rid of the competition of another which lay between them, they went to work on a canal that would deflect the river's waters.

Craft specialization, however, supplied a more effective means for a city to compete with the others. Every city was able to supply a great variety of goods to its district, but Lucca made the best silks, Brescia had an edge in arms manufacturing, Bologna provided huge quantities of shoes, Cremona was famous for inexpensive "fustians" (textiles of cotton mixed with wool). Milan alone established her renown on being proficient at almost everything, much as Philadelphia in the early stages of American industrialization. Again, every city tried to attract skilled workers from other cities while forbidding her own to bring their skills elsewhere. Industry, like commerce, was less diversified outside Italy, and some of the best items had to be imported by itinerant merchants such as the "mercers," but in Italy even the smallest towns often had well-stocked shops and at least one specialty of their own.

DEPOSIT BANKING AND
FINANCE AS AN OFFSHOOT
OF TRADE

Credit organization was another tool of commercial competition. We have seen that although credit was normally involved in all but the smallest operations of trade, its development as a specialized profession was fairly slow even in Italy. Indeed, medieval banking in its more powerful manifestations remained an offshoot of commerce.

Pawnbrokers, of course, existed nearly everywhere, but their methods and interest rates were not adjusted to the needs of legitimate commerce. Most deposit bankers were natives of towns of the interior: Asti and Piacenza in the Po valley had an early lead but were soon joined by a number of Tuscan towns; Florence and Siena gained prominence. Southern France, too, had in Cahors an internationally famous center of deposit banking. Even the most successful members of the profession, however, did not have sufficient reserves in the twelfth and thirteenth centuries to compete with the great international merchants as financial backers of large commercial ventures. The comparatively moderate interest they charged made them especially useful to craftsmen and petty traders but limited their chances to build up their capital. Moreover, the growth of deposit banking was braked in two utterly different directions. On the one hand, municipal regulations usually raised the bankers to the status of auxiliary supervisors of currency and the money market but endeavored to insure their solvency by submitting their operations to special controls. On the other hand, ecclesiastic tribunals did not distinguish commercial interest from usury and lent assistance to any unscrupulous borrower who wished to fool his banker (at least once!) by refusing to pay back anything but the original amount of a freely contracted interest-bearing loan.

What ordinary deposit bankers could not do came easier to international merchants engaging in the banking business as a side activity. Whether or not they formally registered as deposit bankers, merchants could legitimately practice the same credit operations in connection with their trade: they accepted interest-bearing deposits, extended loans at higher interest rates, and, above all, took full advantage of instruments or letters of exchange to charge whatever interest they wished without incurring the censure of the Church. These letters were contracts whereby a party received from another an advance in local currency and promised repayment in another currency and another place. Ostensibly the main purpose was to provide the second party with foreign money abroad while saving him the risk and expense of taking along an equivalent amount of local currency; if this was the case, as it may well have been at an early stage, the first party would have been entitled to a service charge for changing the currency and taking care of the transfer. Since the local currency was paid in advance, however, and repayment was delayed until the letter or the second party had reached his destination, the transaction actually involved a loan by the second party to the first, for which the first party was charged an interest easily concealed in a doctored-up rate of exchange. Even the difference of currency and place could be eliminated by a second contract or a clause reversing the operation (that is, arranging for a transfer of the foreign currency back to the original place and in the original currency). The latter, fairly transparent trick (*ricorsa* or "dry exchange"), however, was not indispensable for a large merchant company whose business called for a continuous flow of payments back and forth from the same place, the Champagne fairs for instance. Already known to both deposit bankers and merchants of the late twelfth century (and probably earlier), the letter of exchange became the most widely used instrument of credit in the course of the thirteenth, as its flexibility was increased by the intensification of overland trade and as its advantages to hide interest charges became more obvious. For the latter purpose, exchange clauses also were grafted into the sea loan contract, but maritime trade utilized them more sparingly because the short-term *commenda* contract met many of its needs in an unimpeachable way.

Although the letter of exchange, like other business techniques, gradually spread throughout the Mediterranean world, large-scale credit based on it became the specialty of a small number of Italian merchant "companies" which rapidly grew to what may be called, in comparison with the average size of inland enterprises, colossal proportions. Unlike sea traders, they could not back their economic penetration with military might; but they used credit grants as a weapon to pry commercial concessions from foreign governments, concessions as a lubricant to get their import and export trade rolling, trade as a means to increase their owned or borrowed capital, capital as prop for further credit grants. Almost paradoxically, the most valuable friend of these companies, which depended so heavily on "usury sins," was the Pope. He badly needed their services in transferring tributes and wares from and to the remotest corners of Europe, and could not afford to look closely into the canonic orthodoxy of their methods; on the contrary, he was ever willing to recommend their partners to Catholic princes and, in extreme cases, to threaten ecclesiastic punishment on debtors who refused to pay.

Nevertheless, the congenital fragility of *compagnia* partnerships made the largest companies most vulnerable. Princes were notoriously bad payers. Joint and unlimited liability, which Siena and other cities tried in vain to make less stringent, placed a tremendous responsibility on every one of the numerous partners. Discord among partners brought down in 1298 the Bonsignori company of Siena, then probably Europe's largest dispenser of credit. Two years later, the death of Gandolfo Arcelli, the wealthiest taxpayer in Paris where he managed the business of the Borrino company of Piacenza, caused the precipitous decline of the partnership. Between then and 1346 one Florentine *compagnia* after another failed. The most powerful among them (Bardi) in 1318 had balanced its books on a figure of about 875,000 florins, more than six times the amount for which some years later the king of France bought Montpellier from her lord; it failed in 1346 without recovering credits of more than a million florins on the kings of England and Sicily. The magnitude of these figures, however, bears witness to the ability of credit to multiply itself.

FROM GREENLAND TO PEKING:
THE EXPLOSION OF
ITALIAN TRADE

In spite of business failures, mounting taxation, piracy, wars, uneven distribution of wealth, and other disturbing factors, the thirteenth century completed for northern and central Italy, and to a lesser degree for the rest of Mediterranean Europe, the transition from inadequate or insecure supply to affluence (in medieval terms at least). Never before had such a large proportion of the population been free from want, or such a variety and abundance of goods been constantly available—not in ancient Rome at its peak, not in Byzantine and Islamic countries at their best. People complained about ever-rising prices, but earnings generally went up still faster, and almost anything could be had at a price. If a harvest failed somewhere, ships could promptly import grain from another country. If a war or an embargo obstructed a source of fine cloth, an order at the Champagne fairs could get much the same cloth from another producer. Even the chronic shortage of metallic currency—a greater nuisance for ordinary customers than for businessmen who could pay by transfer orders on their bank accounts or letters of exchange—was alleviated when Genoa issued fine gold genoins in 1252, Florence followed suit a few months later with her gold florins of the same weight, and many other communal and royal mints took similar steps after a while. We need not discuss the intricate and controversial interpretations of the background of the reform; probably the decisive, though not the sole factor was a steep rise in the price of silver, which in 1252 momentarily exceeded one-tenth of the price of gold. The new gold coins released much silver for ordinary payments, provided a stable international currency in the midst of wild debasement and chaotic diversity, and advertised the economic superiority of Italy over the declining Byzantine and Muslim countries whose gold reserves were dwindling.

The problems of plenty are different from those of scarcity. No great modifications were needed in the basic contracts that had served the merchants in the age of high risks, small markets, and thin competition, but adjustments had to be made to the fact that the number of sellers had increased in proportion to that of buyers, and efficiency rather than daring would lead to success on a diminished profit margin. We have mentioned the organization of convoys to make voyages safer; but it still was expedient for isolated ships to take chances, and travel risks could best be separated from commercial risks by making insurance, like banking, a specialized profession. Progress was slower, because insurance can hardly differ from gambling so long as it is not subdivided among very many insurers and spread over very many ships; but we can watch the first meandering experiments in the late thirteenth century, and by the early fourteenth Genoa and Florence are distinctly in the lead. They also seem to be ahead of other Italian towns in the evolution of commercial and banking accounting, which gradually changes from scribbled memos to separate columns for credit and debt, and ultimately to rigorous double entry bookkeeping of the kind that is still used (with the help of computers) today. These tools greatly helped a merchant to keep track of involved business, check the operations of his partners and agents, and learn from the past how to plan for the future. More literary or scientific tools, ranging from manuals of commerce to maps, will be considered briefly when we take a look at the impact of the Commercial Revolution on culture, an impact that was felt earlier and more sharply in Italy than in the other Mediterranean countries.

Perhaps the most striking by-product of growing maturity was the consolidation of colonies and the increasing reliance of international traders on quasi-sedentary agents abroad. Some economic historians, looking at the past in modern perspective, have saluted what they called "the advent of the sedentary merchant" as a sudden, revolutionary change, which made business more efficient by eliminating the waste of time and interruption of contacts the "traveling merchant" of old incurred when he boarded a ship or rode a horse instead of sitting behind his desk. This, however, is an oversimplification. Peddlers, like modern traveling salesmen, were always on the move, and ordinary shopkeepers hardly ever had to move; but international merchants had good reasons to alternate office work and business trips. The trips gave them access to the latest news and the best bargains; taking turns with associates and partners saved them much slow and uncomfortable travel, but cut down their profits. Gradually, however, as profit rates went down and access to commercial opportunities broadened, the premium for traveling fell below the cost of travel. An increasing proportion of transactions was carried out by correspondence: ships conveyed messages and contracts back and forth; a weekly courier service from and to the Champagne fairs brought price lists and market analyses to the home offices of Italian partnerships and shuttled back with detailed instructions to local representatives; a growing number of Italian merchants moved their headquarters from their native towns to a permanent outpost abroad.

The move was not always easy. Some foreign cities and princes, wishing to reserve the best opportunities, discouraged immigration by restricting residence permits or hiking taxes on resident aliens; but others were more open-minded or responded to pressure. Colonies, of course, welcomed citizens of their motherland. Their original population was usually made up of younger sons, junior partners, salaried employees and commission agents who speeded back home as soon as they could. As time went by, people of any age settled down in the colony, begat children from local women, and built replicas of their home cities abroad. "So many are the Genoese—so scattered world wide—that they form other Genoas —wherever they reside," said proudly a vernacular poet of the thirteenth century. Each outpost in turn served as a jumping board for further expansion; and even where no colony existed, Italian penetration deepened inside Europe. A Lucchese *compagnia* with branches in France sent agents as far as Greenland to collect papal tithes payable in sealskins, whalebone, and sinews of whales. The Florentine tithe collectors in England gradually displaced the local Jews as credit agents and gatherers of wool from monastic institutions. Money lenders from Asti and Pistoia used their first footholds in Savoy and Burgundy to spread their nets all over France. Central and eastern Europe were less affected, but individual Italians made their way here and there, with trades as different as farming, mining, and importing arbalests.

Greater breakthroughs were achieved by sea. As the Mediterranean got crowded with ships and the demand for goods beyond it pushed prices up, Italian pressure mounted against the political and economic barriers that separated it from the Black Sea, the Red Sea, and the Atlantic Ocean. The first lock was broken in 1204, when the Byzantine Empire, which used to forbid foreigners to sail beyond Constantinople, was temporarily overthrown. First the Venetians, then (as allies of a partially restored Byzantine Empire in 1261) the Genoese established a cluster of colonial outposts all around the Black Sea. Repeated attempts at conquering Egypt and reaching the Red Sea through the Suez bottleneck failed, but the rise of the immense Mongolian Empire, stretching all the way from China to the Russian shores of the Black Sea and the Mediterranean coast of Asia Minor, suddenly disclosed to Italian merchants an immense field of operation. In the course of the thirteenth century virtually the entire continent of Asia, many times larger than Europe—the places of origin of innumerable spices, the greatest sources of silk, the homes of both highly sophisticated nations and utterly primitive tribes, whose combined numbers and resources dwarfed the familiar European scene—was welded together by the terrible, merciless Mongolian might, then transformed into a relatively friendly confederation of four Khanates (Golden Horde, Persia, Turkestan, and China). Here Italian enterprise was welcomed as a counterweight to that of the Arabs, the Hindus, the Chinese, and other traders still smarting under the Mongolian heel.

It took almost the entire century before the followers of Chingiz Khan and his successors changed their policies from brutal warfare to peace and toleration; nor was the change immediately evident to the frightened Europeans. Uncommon perceptiveness and flexibility enabled the Italian merchants (first the Genoese and the Venetians, then traders from inland cities) to realize that by trusting the Mongolians they could bypass the Arab intermediaries of Far Eastern trade and travel safely over virtually unknown lands towards the coveted, fabulous wealth of the "Indies," under which name the Westerners used to lump together all countries beyond the Islamic Middle East. Marco Polo, the Venetian, is but one of many who picked up the challenge between the second half of the thirteenth century and the first half of the fourteenth. His book made him alone deservedly famous. It must not cause us to overlook the rank and file of merchants whom commercial contracts

The Mongolian Empire
(with Italian Itineraries and Atlantic routes)

and narrative sources show motion back and forth from the Mediterranean to Peking or to Zayton, the seaport opposite Formosa on the Chinese mainland, where a miniature colony of Italian merchants took root for a short time. Other merchants, after reaching Turkestan from South Russia or Asia Minor and Persia, crossed the Mongolian border into Delhi, the capital of the largest Muslim state in India. A much larger number did not go that far, but made Tabriz in Persia, Sarai on the Volga River, and even Urgench in Central Asia (the namesake of organdi cloth) as familiar as were Constantinople and Alexandria a century earlier. Genoese shipbuilders, hired or protected by the Khan of Persia, sailed the Caspian Sea and the Persian Gulf. The most daring attempt, however, was one that failed: in 1291 two Genoese brothers, Ugolino and Vadino Vivaldi, loaded two galleys with merchandise and crossed the strait of Gibraltar with the intention of reaching "the Indies" by a "westward route" (that of Columbus or that of Vasco da Gama?—the documents are not clear on this point), but they never came back.

The Italian penetration into the Asiatic continent was much more than a collection of isolated adventures. Its practical importance is stressed in a few pages of Pegolotti's manual of commerce, which describe minutely the northernmost route, from the Crimea to Peking, as one that was "perfectly safe by day and night." Yet even that route, which could be covered in about nine months, entailed expenses and risks that severely restricted its attractiveness. It paid to export directly to China the finest French and German linen and to bring back China silk, because the price differential outweighed the cost of those light, valuable wares, but other commodities could be exchanged only along shorter stretches of the route, as was the custom for inland trade in Europe. Another route, from Asia Minor and Persia to India or China, was somewhat shorter but riskier. A route entirely by sea from the Persian Gulf along the shores of the Indian Ocean, was comparatively cheaper but took more than two years. Obviously the capital and, above all, the manpower of the Italians were not adequate for a thorough exploitation of their opportunities in Asia, but if we consider the similarly inadequate means with which the Portuguese and the Spaniards in the sixteenth century began their expansion in the eastern and western "Indies," the potential of the earlier Italian expansion will look strong enough.

A nearer, and hence more easily exploited frontier lay beyond the strait of Gibraltar. Originally the keys of the passage between the Mediterranean and the Atlantic belonged to the Muslims, who controlled Morocco and Granada; but even before a Castilian-Genoese fleet broke the Moroccan sea power in 1293 the lock had never been too tight for individual ships to go through. As early as the twelfth century the Genoese began sailing south along the Moroccan coast, looking above all for mysterious "Palola," the Senegalese region from where much gold came at a low price. They cautiously lengthened their routes during the thirteenth century and reached the Canary Islands in the early fourteenth. Then the Portuguese and to a smaller extent the Castilians and French took over the lead in the step-by-step exploration of the southern Atlantic, which was to produce its greatest dividends in the fifteenth century with Vasco da Gama. In the period with which we are concerned, however (before 1350), the most momentous maritime expansion was not along the southern but the northern Atlantic coast. Unlike the African sea lanes, which persistent legends populated with monsters and filled with terrors, the European sea lanes from Gibraltar to Flanders and England were not frightening for the Mediterranean sailors. Economic considerations, however, long dissuaded Italian seamen from competing with the Portuguese, Castilian, Basque, French, English, Flemish, and Dutch seamen who ploughed the Atlantic with smaller ships and over shorter stretches. Italian trade went north more cheaply by land routes through the Alps.

Between the end of the thirteenth century and the beginning of the fourteenth, however, the Genoese and the Venetians found ways to transport their wares more cheaply over direct sea routes to La Rochelle, Southampton and Bruges by combining precious and bulky wares more ingeniously on galleys that were enlarged enough to increase their payload, yet not too much to impair their speed. The first convoys that reached the North Sea from Venice and Genoa around 1315 determined the virtual annexation of the northern Atlantic coast of Europe to the Mediterranean sphere of influence and transferred to the Italians a large proportion of the foreign trade of England, France, and the Low Countries. Beyond these points, however, navigation from the Mediterranean became too circuitous to be competitive with land routes through the Alps. The northern seas remained the preserve of northern sailors.

THE NORTHERN MEDITERRANEAN

We have already pointed out the broad physical analogy between the classic Mediterranean and the long arm of the Ocean that stretches from the eastern British coast to the dead ends of the Baltic. Germany occupies its middle, with the Jutland peninsula protruding northwards much as Italy protrudes southward at the center of the Mediterranean; the location of Lübeck and Hamburg, at the root of the peninsula, may be roughly compared to that of Venice and Genoa at the root of Italy. Some analogy can also be detected between the historical processes that led to Italian predominance in the southern Mediterranean and German predominance in the northern seas.

In Germany as in Italy, the agricultural revival and military recovery from the tenth century on enabled a number of towns to develop their local and long-distance trade, to challenge the authority of the emperor and his vassals, and eventually to build up a commercial and colonial empire. Trade was the main driving force, but economic penetration often was supported by the sword. Again, as in Italy, some of the towns that played a prominent role in the early period—Cologne, Mainz, and Ratisbon above all— were old Roman centers where a trickle of trade had never ceased flowing, if only because a resident bishop or lay lord maintained a cluster of potential consumers within their walls. They were joined, however, by new urban nodes and episcopal sees sprouting in the wake of the German eastward expansion under the Carolingians and their successors: Bremen, Hamburg, and Magdeburg, like Venice and Amalfi, were children of the Middle Ages. Even the internal structure of the urban society in the early period of expansion, so far as we can tell through a much scantier documentation than that of Italy, was not unlike that of many Italian towns.

Closely knit groups of interrelated families (the "patricians," as
modern historians rather improperly call them) all but monopolized
public offices; they also were leaders in long-distance trade and
owned much land, including valuable plots around the market
place. Some of their ancestors may well have been petty noblemen
who felt the attraction of trade.

Analogies, however, go no farther than this. The German urban
development was slower than the Italian one and did not attain
as much. Not before 1288 did Cologne finally break the power of
her archbishop in the battle of Worringen, and to achieve that
goal she needed the help of other feudal lords; still the archbishop
and other vassals continued to rule over most of her district.
Hemmed in and often harassed by the territorial princes in their
vicinity, the German towns generally had to settle for something
less than the rugged independence and all-pervasive commercialism
of the Italian communes. They invited imperial protection and,
finding it inadequate, often huddled together in regional leagues.
They let lingering feudal and agrarian interest weaken the main
commercial and industrial bent of the urban community. As a partial compensation for the resulting mediocrity of their economic
and political progress, they were spared some of the dramatic business crises and fierce conflicts that filled with tension the urban
history of Italy. Moreover, the relations between merchants and
princes did not have to be unfriendly; common interests in Germany produced remarkable instances of collaboration. As early as
1120 the duke of Zähringen joined twenty-four prominent merchants in founding Freiburg-im-Breisgau, and the same pattern
was followed in the foundation of Bern. Prolonged collaboration
with princes was instrumental in Germany's greatest urban success,
the formation of what was eventually to be called the Hanseatic
League.

Hansa, it must be noted, was a term commonly used in northern
Europe, chiefly but not exclusively to designate associations of
merchants; its original meaning probably was "armed convoy,"
which appropriately describes the military underpinning of trade.
Long before the thirteenth century several hansas appeared and
disappeared at different points along or near the southern coast of
the North Sea; but the Hanseatic League "par excellence" was

founded only in 1369, when Cologne and other Rhinish towns joined a preexisting, informal alliance of German seaports of the "northern Mediterranean." This alliance, however, was the crowning product of the relentless commercial and military expansion of Germanic people from the ninth century on. In the ninth and early tenth centuries, when the prowess and seamanship of the Vikings dominated the entire northern world, only the Frisians, a hardy folk of peasant-traders living between Rhine and Weser, dared to compete with the Scandinavians. With less primitive methods Westphalian merchants carried forward the challenge between Weser and Elbe in the late tenth and early eleventh centuries, but did not yet threaten the Scandinavian predominance in the Baltic. The tide began to turn in 1143, when Lübeck, originally a Slavonic settlement whose ruler had welcomed German settlers but had succumbed to the aggression of a German lord, was founded again as a wholly German town by Henry the Lion, the cousin and rival of Frederic Barbarossa.

Lübeck, placed on the eastern side of the narrow neck of land that separated the Baltic from Hamburg and the North Sea, was ideally located to serve as the master link between the two halves of the northern Mediterranean while the Scandinavians still had the Jutland straits firmly in their grip. For more than one century after her second foundation two co-belligerent drives caught almost all of the southern Baltic and its hinterland into a net. German merchants hopping from one river mouth or natural harbor to another used their naval and commercial proficiency to found a series of towns, all of which looked upon Lübeck as the kingpin of their trade and the ancestral home of their leading families. German knights sweeping through the inland plains used their superior armament and organization to crush the resistance of thinly settled Slavs and Balts, and made the wilderness alive with settlements of peasants brought in from as far as Westphalia and Flanders. Ever since the beginning the German advance into pagan or scarcely Christian countries had been wrapped in vaguely religious colors; it became officially a crusade in Latvia and Estonia, where the Teutonic Order of knights preceded or assisted the merchants with its remarkable combination of ruthless force and business talent. Lithuania alone resisted to the end. Poland and Russia,

The Northern Mediterranean

which had long been Christian and fairly well developed, held out against conquest but welcomed commercial penetration. A belated attempt by the Danes to stop German penetration failed. By 1274 Reval, originally a Danish outpost in Estonia which had been subsequently absorbed into the German sphere, could write to Lübeck: "Our two towns belong together like the arms of Christ crucified." Theirs was a silver cross, wrought of German conquering trade.

As a matter of fact, between the late eleventh and the late thirteenth centuries the Scandinavian military and economic power collapsed. No doubt the merging of the Scandinavian elites with much larger native populations in Russia, Normandy, and southern Italy was an inevitable consequence of overexpansion; so was the fall of the Viking possessions in the British Isles. But the contraction of their power in their home waters of the northern Mediterranean calls for still another explanation, especially as their unruly tribes at the same period should have gained strength through consolidation into the three kingdoms of Denmark, Norway, and Sweden. Indeed the king of Norway brought under his control the remote, poverty-stricken Scandinavian communities in Greenland and Iceland; the king of Sweden annexed peripheral Finland; but the vigorous campaigns of several Danish kings could not for long prevent the Germans from evicting the Danes from their once extensive domains on the southern and eastern Baltic shores. Again, the Scandinavian "brotherhood" of merchants at Visby in the central Baltic island of Gotland was eclipsed by the community of "German visitors of Gotland," which was the first core of the future Hanseatic League. More than that, by a combination of diplomacy and warfare the German merchants gained special privileges at the great fairs of Skanör (in the Danish-dominated part of southern Sweden), in all ports of the Swedish kingdom, and in all those of Norway except the extreme north.

All told, the German pattern of penetration into the Scandinavian sphere of influence and home ports resembled that of the Italian merchants on Byzantine and Islamic shores. Like the Greeks and the Muslims, though in a much more primitive context, the Scandinavians were early starters who failed to keep up with economic and social progress. Sea trade with them was not so much the business of free townsmen as that of noblemen and peasants with a knack for navigation. Their ships, which had supplied models to all northern peoples, were now smaller than the German cog, a sturdy sailship fitted for the bulkiest cargoes. They lagged behind the Germans in replacing the traditional lateral rudders with a central rudder, more effective to steer ponderous ships. All of their commercial techniques were getting out of date.

Let us not infer that the "Easterlings" (as German traders were then called in England; the suggestion that the pound sterling may have borrowed its name from them is a seductive but improbable guess) had caught up with Italian or Catalan techniques. It was enough for them to be more advanced than their competitors in the northern seas. Their versions of the partnership and *commenda* contracts, possibly derived from still simpler Scandinavian models, were cruder and hazier than their Mediterranean counterparts. Double-entry accounting and insurance were totally unknown. Credit organization was rudimentary, although commercial interest rates in Lübeck became as low as in Italy and the bankruptcy of Hermann Clendenst in 1335 shook the town as thoroughly as the contemporary bank failures in Florence. Literacy was fairly widespread, but not as much as among Italian or Belgian burghers. The cities of the Easterlings in the course of the thirteenth century became nearly as independent as the Italian communes, but their ruling classes were more closed, and the hinterland, as that of the Catalan ports, escaped their control. On the other hand, the Easterlings were less embroiled than the Italians in party strife, mutual competition, and fights for oversea empires. They generally avoided inter-city rivalry by accepting Lübeck's leadership, and reduced the quest for permanent colonies by shuttling rapidly across narrow stretches of sea and back to home ports. One establishment at the eastern end of their longest route—the "yard" at Novgorod, which they captured from the Scandinavians—and three at the outer prongs of the western end—the "steelyard" at London, the "kontor" at Bruges, and the autonomous quarter at Bergen—took care of most of their oversea needs. Even here their holdings were no larger than the earliest Italian enclaves: the establishments and privileges were permanent, but the population consisted chiefly of temporary callers, and sovereignty rested with the local rulers.

Most of the objects of German sea trade reflected a less developed economy than that of the classic Mediterranean. Oriental spices and refined wares, which for a short time around the tenth century had reached Scandinavia through the Russian rivers, now came to Germany from the west, as did other luxuries of French and Italian origin. The demand, however, was limited to the fairly small number of people who could appreciate and afford them. Far more important was the flow of raw materials from Russia, Poland, and the new and old German hinterland: rye, grain, timber, pitch, tar, honey, wax, and furs. More timber, pitch, and tar came from Scandinavia. Bohemia and Hungary sent some of their precious and non-precious metals; England, her wool and hides. The odor of salted herring, less sweet but more substantial than that of spices, dominated the scene. Without the salt of nearby Lüneburg, Lübeck might never have risen above mediocrity, but she soon had to supplement it with French and Portuguese salt. The herring trade had its main center at the Skanör fairs: the king of Denmark still collected tolls and his subjects unloaded the fish, but the Lübeck merchants were the most important buyers. We lack figures for our period, but by 1368 their purchases came close to 34,000 barrels and rose steadily thereafter. In conclusion, the list of commodities included very few noble items, but it missed none of the basic necessities of life.

IN A LOWER KEY

International trade was by no means an Italian and Easterling monopoly: the economic and political unification of Europe, which is still far from achieved today, would have been absolutely unthinkable in the Middle Ages. By the early fourteenth century only the Catalans withheld from the Italians a significant share of long distance commerce in the classic Mediterranean, and only the English and Dutch held their own in the western corner of the northern Mediterranean, but many bulky goods of the Atlantic regions, such as Gascon wine and Basque iron, were still transported mainly by local ships, and short-haul navigation was everybody's business. All but a fraction of the goods produced far from the sea were forwarded to the surrounding regions and to the main commercial collection centers by local merchants.

In these backwaters and inner recesses of Europe, business tended to be carried out in a lower key: capital, credit, turnover, organization, and the size of individual enterprises were generally smaller than with the Italians and the Easterlings. There were, however, substantial differences from place to place. France, which was in the forefront of agricultural progress and productivity, and fairly proficient in many crafts, played a very modest role in long-distance trade. Provence and Languedoc, which had made some progress at an early time in Mediterranean trade, found it difficult to keep up with the Italians in the thirteenth century and tended to lean more heavily on specialized crops such as wine and woad (a dyestuff). At the same period, Flanders was driven by the very success of her textile industries to concentrate all efforts in that field. Almost none of the other French regions suffered from the dramatic food shortages that almost forced the Italians to become merchants; taxation, weighed in favor of agricultural interests, absorbed a large proportion of available surpluses, and what was left sufficed to invite foreign merchants who supplied whatever goods might still be desired from other countries. We have seen that in 1292 an Italian merchant banker headed the list of taxpayers in Paris (noblemen and clergymen were exempt); five of the six who followed him also were Italian. The only Frenchman was Pierre Marcel, probably an ancestor of Etienne Marcel, who was provost of the merchants and a leader of the revolution of 1365. Add that long dynasties of merchants, such as those which ruled the Italian communes, were extremely rare: in medieval France, as in ancient Rome, enriched businessmen more often than not withdrew from trade the best part of their profits, bought land and a title of nobility, and placed their sons in the service of the king.

Much the same pattern prevailed in England, but the proximity of the sea to most of her territory and a smaller diversification of local production and crafts increased the attraction of trade. International exchanges throve on England's surpluses of wool and thirst for wine. The comparative backwardness of commercial and credit organization forced the English merchants to depend heavily on the Jews and, after these were squeezed dry and expelled, on Italian merchant bankers. Still, though foreigners aggressively competed for all commercial opportunities, the king, one of the few western sovereigns to exercise effective economic control over his realm, endeavored to reserve for English ships and traders a substantial share. Catalan merchants, too, leaned heavily on royal support and made the most of it; but the kingdom of Aragon was not as productive as England, and the inertia of the feudal hinterland slowed down the spirited activity of Barcelona and other seaports.

Backwardness, however, was by no means an unsurmountable impediment to active or, at least, passive international trade while commercialization engulfed one region after another. In the crowning phase of the Commercial Revolution (thirteenth and early fourteenth centuries) some of the late starters caught up with many early risers that had failed to gain momentum. Castile and Portugal, having almost completed the reconquest of the Iberian peninsula from the Muslims, began to wake up to the great opportunities available to them on the high seas. Increased production of metals and intensified use of their internal river system enabled southern Germany, Austria, and Bohemia to insert themselves in the mainstream of long distance trade, using Venice, Cologne, and Vienna as their ultimate links with the two Mediterraneans and the Orient. Farther east, Poland and Serbia channeled their commerce to sea through such ports as Gdansk on the Baltic and Dubrovnik (Ragusa) on the Adriatic. Even Russia, which had lost long before her southern provinces to invaders from Asia (the Petchenegs and, later, the Cumans), was still more seriously handicapped when the tremendous power of the Mongolians established itself firmly in the south and submitted to its overlordship the rest of the country. International trade did not come to a full stop, but had to be channeled mostly through the Genoese and Venetian Black Sea colonies or through Russia's Baltic outpost of Novgorod, a city-state allied with the Easterlings.

As for other early risers who lost speed, we shall not linger on the economic decline of the Byzantine and the Muslims, whose homes were beyond the confines of Catholic Europe, but we cannot leave the Jews entirely unmentioned. The twelfth and thirteenth centuries were a period of increased religious awareness and militancy at all levels of society; moreover, all governments strengthened their hold on their subjects; further, the numbers, proficiency, and organization of native traders made progress throughout Catholic Europe. All this was bound to reduce the acceptability and usefulness of alien minorities within the fold. Even the Italian financiers, who were not "infidel" and enjoyed the protection of the Pope as well as that of their states, occasionally suffered confiscations and other harassment in thirteenth- and fourteenth-century France and England. The Jews fared much worse. They were gradually crowded out of honorable commerce and herded into the highly dangerous lines of business that would make them hated because of their ruthlessness and ruthless because of the hate they encountered. No doubt there continued to be princes and towns that needed the Jews, whether for respectable or disreputable operations; and the general expansion of economic opportunities may on the whole have caused the absolute size of their transactions to grow. Nevertheless, their proportional share in the benefits of the Commercial Revolution tended to become ever more marginal and insecure.

5

Between Crafts and Industry

MERCHANTS AND CRAFTSMEN

The Industrial Revolution has so radically altered the relation between merchant and industrialist, that it takes some effort for us to realize how crucially important the capital, credit, connections, and initiative of merchants could be for the development of medieval crafts. Like his Roman counterpart, the medieval artisan tended to be the prisoner of a closed circle: he produced little because he had inadequate tools, and had inadequate tools because he did not produce fast enough to gather capital and invest it in mechanization. His horizons, too, were limited by his small productivity: he had neither the means nor the incentive to enlarge his operations by massive borrowing and hiring, or to broaden his market by searching for customers beyond his immediate reach. Whatever industrial growth had occurred in antiquity was due primarily to the interest that government officials and affluent landowners had in provisioning themselves; still the craftsmen, whether they were slaves or freemen, seldom rose to a high material and social standing, and if they did, usually hastened to change profession or live as gentlemen on unearned income. The early Middle Ages promoted slave artisans to serf status and occasionally paid lip service to the moral nobility of labor—were not St. Joseph and all the apostles laborers?—but offered no fresh opportunities for industrial development. From the tenth century on,

however, the rise of the merchant class brought forth a new source
of potential support. As middlemen between supply and demand,
merchants had a personal stake in the expansion of both; they had
capital, extended credit, and promoted their business through
market research. No unsurmountable prejudice separated them
from craftsmen: many if not all of them originally came from the
same social background, and the struggle for urban emancipation
from feudal control supplied a common cause, in the eleventh and
twelfth centuries at least.

Still we must consider that wealth created rank among merchants,
and that birth and profession, too, played a significant role. A
petty trader born of undistinguished parents would be pleased to
befriend an established artisan and perhaps to marry his daughter,
but could do little to help the artisan's workshop. On the other
hand an affluent, esteemed businessman would respect a goldsmith
and possibly a master shipwright, but often looked down upon
ordinary craftsmen, almost in the same way as great noblemen
looked down upon ordinary merchants. This need not have prevented him from backing a dependable artisan in many ways, by
ordering goods and paying in advance, by granting loans for the
purchase of raw materials and tools, or merely by finding and sug-
gesting new markets and methods. The relationship between a rich
trader and an impecunious producer, however, lacked the spirit of
solidarity that characterized agreements between fellow merchants,
even when one of the parties had all of the money and the other
contributed only his work. At worst, a merchant might take advantage of the craftsman's economic inferiority to charge him an exorbitant interest or underpay his products. At best, he gave the
craftsman a fair deal but not enough credit to buy elaborate machinery or stock up raw materials for future expansion. Deposit
bankers were often more willing to extend credit to artisans, but
they had limited resources and could not take chances as freely as
merchant bankers or great merchants.

Yet commerce and industry were strictly related. Most artisans
were part-time traders, since they sold some of their products directly to the public. High quality work on valuable materials, fast
production of simpler wares for mass consumption, or even ex-
traneous factors such as a full warehouse in a besieged city, a nest

egg lent to needy colleagues, or a marriage with a woman of property could transform a craftsman into a merchant entrepreneur, who did not toil with his own hands but sold the handicraft of others. Conversely, most merchants traded not only in unprocessed foodstuffs and raw materials, but also in manufactured goods. A merchant whose business depended heavily on the products of a craft might invest in it a considerable proportion of his capital and labor and become a part-time or full-time craft entrepreneur.

CRAFT GUILDS

While lagging behind the dynamism of trade, medieval industry was by no means immobile; nor was its average mediocrity without compensating factors. Craftsmen shared the benefits which the Commercial Revolution, and the agricultural progress on which it was based, generally bestowed upon the middle and lower classes from the tenth century on: more food, better communications, relief from the worst forms of personal bondage, some labor-saving devices, and, above all, expanding opportunities. No doubt we often hear of ruthless exploitation of the lower ranks by usurers and entrepreneurs; but the relentless, ubiquitous immigration of apprentices and laborers looking for employment in the workshops of every town seems to indicate that working conditions were more attractive in the urban crafts than on the fields—be it only because no village could match the variety of occupations, distractions, and hopes available even in the sleepiest towns.

Beside offering freedom to the serf and social mobility to the free, towns gave to a growing number of people a chance to join the urban guilds. These, like the merchant guilds of various kinds that appeared in many towns between the tenth century and the twelfth, were professional associations that tried to monopolize a branch of trade and to promote its interests. Craft guilds, however, had a longer life and usefulness than the merchant guilds, which after a while merged into the government of merchants that was the commune, or degenerated into cliques of big businessmen and of petty tradesmen. They also differed from merchant guilds in two essential ways. Whereas merchant guilds accepted members on a foot of equality but allowed each of them to tip the balance in his favor by pursuing unlimited gains, craft guilds brought together employers and employees, masters and apprentices as unequal partners, but strove to insure for all members an equal chance of advancement and success.

The balance was maintained by curbing the inclination of any member to grab more than his share of the business. As a matter of fact, craft guilds reflected the modest possibilities of feebly capitalized and mechanized workshops, whose owners could hardly reach for unlimited gain without overworking their dependents or crowding out their colleagues. They functioned at their best in small towns, where security was more desirable than opportunity, or in those larger cities that were consumption centers rather than production hubs. Paris, where the butcher's guild eventually became the most powerful among a hundred professional associations or *métiers,* is the outstanding example of the latter kind. The guild structure, however, was elastic enough to fit any urban type and any profession. By 1294 more than 36,000 out of almost 50,000 inhabitants of Bologna were members of a guild or relatives of members, according to a careful extrapolation of fragmentary statistical evidence. Beside 2,000 students and 1,500 members of the clergy, less than 10,000 people were either too high or too low to be included in a guild structure that in Bologna covered not only craftsmen and shopkeepers but also such professional men as notaries and physicians.

To return to craft guilds proper, they easily attained their goals, security and balance, with a stable number of members sharing fairly stable opportunities. They could adjust their rules to moderate, steady growth, but fast economic growth subjected them to a strain. Insofar as they succeeded in regulating growth without stopping it, they spared their humbler members the extreme sufferings that were inflicted on the slave gangs of antiquity and the factory hands of the early Industrial Revolution. Their braking action, however, tended to maintain the entire craft at an economic level closer to Greco-Roman "golden mediocrity" than to the moving escalators of modern industrial capitalism.

We shall not try to compare the craft guilds that arose from the tenth century on and attained their fullest development in the thirteenth (but even then did not cover all people in all crafts) to the ancient and early medieval organizations that preceded them and in some cases probably engendered them; such problems of origin are highly controversial and blurred by the lack of adequate evidence. Even for the period of the Commercial Revolution we must depend for information on flexible customary rules or, at best, fragmentary and often contradictory statements; moreover, certain activities of the craft guilds were illegal, and the guilds themselves often had a long clandestine existence before obtaining official recognition. Fully codified by-laws can be found mostly for the period after 1300, and experience has shown that they must not be read back into the twelfth and thirteenth centuries. The main lines of the craft guilds' internal structure, however, are clear enough.

A guild was a federation of autonomous workshops, whose owners (the masters) normally made all decisions and established the requirements for promotion from the lower ranks (journeymen or hired helpers, and apprentices). Inner conflicts were usually minimized by a common interest in the welfare of the craft and a virtual certitude that sooner or later every proficient apprentice and industrious journeyman would become a master and share in the governance of the craft. To make sure that expectations would be fulfilled, a guild would normally forbid overtime work after dark and sometimes limit the number of dependents a master could employ; this also served to maintain substantial equality among masters and to prevent overexpansion of the craft. The latter danger, however, did not become serious before the second half of the fourteenth century. So long as the prospects for sustained growth remained open, there were none of the unreasonable restrictions that gave a bad name to later guilds: it was fairly easy for an outsider to obtain admission, for a master to enlarge his staff, for an apprentice to qualify as a master. At worst, a dissatisfied craftsman could bring his skill to another town; though guilds and town governments endeavored to forbid emigration of experienced artisans, they seldom could prevent a fugitive from being welcomed elsewhere. Guilds often stressed their concern for producing good wares at low prices; their statements to that effect should be neither disbelieved nor overrated. Then, as now, the main object of a producer could not be to serve God and the public, but to sell his goods at a profit; still he knew that shoddy goods at inflated prices would not keep him in business. The religious, patriarchal character of guilds and the pressure of what was essentially a buyer's market were mutually reinforcing influences; it is idle to debate which one was stronger.

Though craft guilds had to present a subdued, benevolent image in a milieu that looked with suspicion at associations of humbler people, their outer structure embodied, in a rudimentary way, some features of both the cartel and the labor union. In order to bolster the economic potential of individual workshops without destroying their autonomy, each guild endeavored to represent the entire membership as a united front. First of all, it tried to standardize the quality, size, and price of its typical products. This helped not only to prevent underselling by unfair competitors (whether within or outside the guild) and underpaying by greedy wholesalers, but also to place the wider reputation of the collectivity behind each master. Inasmuch as advertising was not an accepted practice, and some medieval regulations even forbade an artisan to attract attention to his products with a nod or a sneeze, the certifying seal of a guild was the best means to bid for distant markets. Only his neighbors might recognize the watermark of a distinguished paper-maker, but Fabriano paper was, and still is, known everywhere. In rather exceptional cases a guild might go so far as to pool the resources of its members in collective purchases of raw materials or collective sales of finished products. These initiatives, however, met with strong resistance in a society obsessed by fear of scarcity and hatred of monopolistic or oligopolistic practices. More often, guilds utilized admission fees and membership dues for a variety of social activities: virtuous ones such as religious ceremonies and assistance to impoverished members, wicked ones such as the bibulous banquets which together with gambling and fornication offered the easiest escape from the monotony of lower middle class life, and dangerous ones such as intervention in political strife.

Before the thirteenth century the ruling merchants usually paid little attention to the demands of craftsmen, although some craftsmen usually held minor offices in the town government. Gradually, however, the disunion of the oligarchs and the growing numbers of guildsmen in the more industrialized cities upset the balance of power. Nevertheless, the first outbursts of popular riots (generally in the first half of the thirteenth century) were often repressed in blood. In the end, however, government by rich merchants was replaced by what was called "government by the people" but turned out to be, more often than not, a mixed rule by both rich and middling merchants and by master artisans of the more substantial crafts. In the major Italian cities the change was generally completed before the end of the thirteenth century; still there was no peace, for other artisans of lower standing began putting pressure to join the ranks of the ruling "people." In Flanders the textile workers triumphed over the French king and the oligarchs at Courtrai (1302) but the subsequent defection of the count, their ally, reduced the effects of their victory; in nearby Brabant they were crushed by the duke at Vilvorde (1306). Elsewhere in Europe "popular" government arose still later, if at all.

Without lingering on political events, let us point out that partial control of the government transferred to privileged categories of artisans or craft entrepreneurs some of the economic advantages that had been previously reserved for the merchants who shaped the policies of their communes without ever forgetting their personal interests. By the same token, however, the continuing exclusion of a larger number of craftsmen widened the economic and social distances that already existed, among and within the crafts, between the rich and the poor. The contrast was not too pronounced inside the humbler crafts, where masters were only a little better off than apprentices, and in the artistic ones, where talent could offset rank. It was sharp, and grew ever sharper, in the broad, diversified industries where masters used their political power to keep subordinate workers and auxiliary craftsmen under their thumb, and entire guilds fell practically under the control of other guilds. To stress the opposition between upper and lower middle classes, some German writers used such transparently biased terms as "the good ones" and "the bad ones." More graphically, the Florentines distinguished "the fat people" from "the thin people." The latter definition, in a city where paupers on welfare lists protested in 1346 because free distributions of white bread had fallen below two pounds a day, may be an overstatement. There is no doubt, how-

ever, that although the delicate balance of the guild system adjusted
fairly well to the slow progress of ordinary crafts, it was easily upset
by the faster acceleration of anything approaching true industrial
growth. Granted that the Commercial Revolution did not immediately produce an industrial revolution, in certain fields it led to
what we might call a "preindustrial rise," that is, more than a craft
but less than an industry of the modern kind.

THE RISE OF
THE WOOLLEN CRAFTS

While commercial expansion and capitalism had their first
medieval successes in luxury trade, where large profits could accrue
from small sales, industrial development could best proceed from
small profits on large sales. Textile industries were not the only
ones that served an essential, universal need—metals, fuels, leather
and hides, pottery and glassware, building and furniture, ships and
other means of transportation were other significant examples—
but they have been pacemakers of industrial progress at least twice
in the last thousand years. As a matter of fact, certain technological
and organizational developments in the cotton industry of the
eighteenth century started the Industrial Revolution that is still
with us; developments of the same kind, if not of the same size, in
the woollen industry of the twelfth century initiated the "preindustrial rise" of the Middle Ages. (One is tempted to look still
further back, and regard some innovating aspects of the Byzantine
and Muslim silk industries before or around the tenth century as
the harbingers of the earliest medieval revival; but we know too
little about that period to express more than a tentative suggestion).

The causes of this consistent priority have never been fully in-
vestigated, but we can suggest some. The production of textiles
easily breaks down into a succession of specialized operations entrusted to separate guilds or working units. The interdependence
of the operations in turn invites reintegration of all units under a
single management. Each operation can be considerably quickened
by fairly simple tools and machinery. The flexibility and light
weight of both the raw materials and the finished products minimize

the impact of transportation costs on the concentration of the manufacturing process wherever cheap labor and initiative are available. The wide range of qualities, costs and, prices of textiles maximizes the range of potential customers. Moderate transportation costs and diversified markets appeal to the merchant capitalists whose help is essential for the transformation of many scattered crafts into one integrated industry.

It is generally agreed that the Industrial Revolution took off in England, where an exceptionally dense population and a high degree of urbanization sustained the internal market, a successful maritime and colonial expansion enlarged the external market, and merchant capitalists were willing to finance the mechanical innovations that radically transformed the cotton industry. It did not matter that cotton fibers were not produced locally; eighteenth-century England was a fertile ground because she bred enterprising men who were somewhat less restrained by class prejudice and rigid regulations than those of most other countries. Not all other countries, however; just across the sea, Holland possessed much the same advantages as England, including a strong tradition in the textile industry, but failed to respond at the crucial moment, possibly because she had a smaller population and had already given all that she could give. These brief remarks about the better known developments of the eighteenth century may be of some help in finding explanations (either by analogy or by contrast) for the less documented preindustrial rise of the Middle Ages. Curiously, the geographic locale was approximately the same, with the two sides of the North Sea playing the opposite role: England was the country that did not make the most of her opportunities, Flanders and the adjacent regions were the ones that did. Italy, which in the Middle Ages had the greatest assets, did not respond at once, although she partly made up for lost time after the mid-thirteenth century; she had her priority not in the woollen industry but in that of silk which was more geared to luxury consumption and Oriental trade.

Let us start from the beginning. As early as the Carolingian period, Flanders (which then included some French-speaking provinces to the south and was closely connected with Brabant and Frisia) was noted for her fine raw wool and dependable textiles. So was England, which raised more sheep and apparently used larger looms to make the extra-long cloaks that shocked the conservative taste of Charlemagne. (While the emperor complained to the king of Mercia about that English extravagance, still longer linen cloth produced by the looms of Naples aroused the admiration of a sophisticated traveler from Baghdad). The demographic explosion of the following centuries, however, pushed the Flemish and the English into opposite yet complementary directions. England, which had land to spare and a demanding feudal monarchy, concentrated her efforts on agriculture and sheep raising, while the textile-producing towns lost momentum. Flanders, where land was scarce and many peasants had to seek a living as far as the German eastern frontier, let pastures be replaced by intensively cultivated plots for the benefit of her growing towns, and turned to commerce and industry. Her development resembled to a certain degree that of Italy in the same period: some members of the lower urban nobility joined a bourgeoisie whose ranks were swollen by immigrant serfs, and feudal government had to make room for a measure of municipal autonomy. The commercial vocation was easily stirred in a country that faced the Strait of Dover and had such neighbors as the Frisian sea merchants and the Meuse river merchants. Ships loaded with continental goods crossed to England and sailed back with the best English wool; other ships, river barges, horses and mules carried Flemish cloth to German markets, the Champagne fairs, and in some instances even as far as Genoa. This movement, which culminated in the second half of the twelfth century, might easily have transformed Flanders into a major commercial power; but it was braked and eventually brought almost to a full stop by the very success of the preindustrial development that was its underpinning. Enough capital had been gathered and invested to insure the success of an industry feeding entirely on imported material; now many merchants became sedentary craft entrepreneurs, while others lent money or just lived off their income. There was no dearth of foreign merchants who would be eager to import wool and export cloth for a profit.

Hindsight tends to justify this turn in the allocation of limited resources. Flanders was too small to bid for primacy both in the woollen industry and in trade; in the latter field she faced stiff competition from larger nations, but in the former, by the thirteenth century, she was far ahead of all rivals, with Italy alone posing a still distant threat. Industry was more manpower-hungry than commerce, in spite of partial mechanization. It absorbed not only entrepreneurs, skilled artisans, and apprentices, but also an ever-rising stream of unskilled country people, who had no elbow room at home and would rather be proletarians in the nearest city than pioneers in the German and Slav far east. We have no exact employment figures, but probably more than half the estimated 50,000 inhabitants that made Ghent the largest city in northwestern Europe drew their livelihood directly or indirectly from the woollen industy. The proportion may have been still higher in Ypres, a slightly smaller city which in 1313 accounted for no less than 40,000 pieces of cloth according to the latest estimates; nearby Louvain and Malines produced about 25,000 pieces each. By way of comparison, Troyes, Champagne's capital, is said to have made barely 2,000 pieces annually; all of England, then facing a depression, exported 4,422 pieces over a twelve-month period in 1347–48). The scale was still vastly inferior to that of the Industrial Revolution, but it had definitely outgrown that of ordinary medieval crafts.

The Belgian cities, moreover, were surrounded by dozens of urban centers in the entire area between the Seine and Rhine, which produced internationally famous woollens on a smaller scale but with similar methods and organization. Florence was getting close to Flemish employment and production figures; many cities in the Po valley turned out cheaper woollens and fustians (of wool and cotton mixed together) for a combined number of pieces that may have exceeded that of Flanders. There was hardly a town in Europe that did not produce some cloth with the simpler, old-fashioned artisan methods.

The rate of mechanization also was halfway between that of ordinary crafts and that of the early stage of the Industrial Revolution. Both in the eighteenth century and in the twelfth the first breakthrough was achieved in the central stages of spinning and weaving, two processes that were so interlocked that acceleration in one of them called for an equal acceleration in the other. The Industrial Revolution went through a rapid succession of mechanical innovations, each of them related to the name of an inventor; the preindustrial rise was content with two simple and inexpensive labor-saving devices, which can neither be dated with precision nor be

assigned to a known inventor: a pedal loom in the place of the
hand loom, and a spinning wheel in the place of the distaff and
spindle. Actually there would have been no technical bar to applying
the already existing power of the water mill to both the spinning

Textile Centers in Europe in the Thirteenth Century

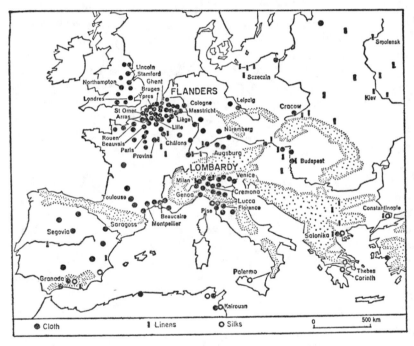

SOURCE: Lopez, *The Birth of Europe,* p. 279. Copyright © 1966 by J. M. Dent &
Sons, Ltd. Reprinted by permission of M. Evans & Co., Inc., and J. M. Dent &
Sons, Ltd.

wheel and the pedal loom, as was done for a while in the Industrial
Revolution. As a matter of fact, by the mid-thirteenth century water
power was applied in Italy to the throwing which prepared the
delicate yarn for the silk industry. Wool yarn, however, was coarser
and cheaper; there was no incentive to invest in a costly machine
while it was possible to put out the wool to underpaid spinstresses.

On the other hand, it paid to equip the "walkers," who pressed and tightened the cloth by trampling upon it, with fulling mills; England's retarded adoption of the machine contributed to her temporary decadence in a craft for which she still produced the finest and most plentiful wool. It also paid to endow dyers with larger vats, shearers with longer scissors, and other specialists with a variety of improved tools; to say nothing of the adoption of better coloring stuffs and mordants, especially for the more valuable grades of woollen. No doubt every new device created hardship for those who did not employ it; the fulling mill, in particular, displaced many "walkers," but in the end mechanization tended to create additional jobs.

In the Middle Ages as in the eighteenth century, but to a smaller degree, division of labor went together with mechanization, and industrial integration restored unified management to the dismembered operations of the craft. There were, however, no factories and no mergers of workshops into large industrial firms. By the mid-thirteenth century we sometimes hear of more than thirty separate steps in the production of cloth, and of almost as many guilds or unorganized but distinct groups of workmen responsible for them. One of the guilds, usually that of the drapers (*drapiers* in French, *lanaioli* in Italian), owned or controlled most of the capital and overlooked all operations from the purchase of raw materials to the marketing of finished products. Whether he came from a family of artisans or from one of merchants, a thirteenth-century draper was hardly a handicraftsman, although he ordinarily had the main skills and might take a hand in the manufacturing of a piece of cloth when he was not too busy supervising it. We may call him an entrepreneur, provided we remember that he had a workshop, not a factory, and that his activity was still encased in the framework of a guild. In the early fourteenth century, about 200 workshops of *lanaioli* had a share in the Florentine cloth production totaling 75,000 pieces a year. Later in the century, Milan had no less than 363 workshops, and the northern drapers' guilds were similarly subdivided. The other guilds, too, consisted of many autonomous units; their members worked in residences they owned or rented, and so did most of the unorganized laborers. Machinery on the whole was not so heavy, and processes not so interdependent, that it would be necessary to herd all workers under one roof; the entrepreneur merely put out the material in succession to each of the craftsmen responsible for a stage of production. By leaving to each subordinate unit the responsibility of running its own business, the drapers saved overhead and made it easier to adjust their orders to the annual and seasonal fluctuations of the market.

A rapid survey of the personnel involved in the Flemish woollen industry will help us understand its stratified structure. On top of the whole organization, not in Flanders alone but in the broader Franco-Belgian area surrounding it, an interurban merchant association, the Hansa of the Seventeen Cities (which by the thirteenth century actually included more than twenty cities) endeavored with mixed effect to coordinate the export of "Francigene cloth" to the fairs of Champagne and other meeting places of foreign traders. Its functions were largely superseded in the fourteenth century, when Bruges, a Flemish city, became the main terminus of shipping from both the classic and the northern Mediterranean thanks to its river port on the Zwyn.

Then there were the drapers, who not only dominated the industry in their native towns but also held important offices in the municipal government. Through political influence, and still more through economic pressure—by expanding or contracting the purchases of raw materials, the orders to the auxiliary guilds and other workers, and the shipping of goods for sale, they regulated to a large extent the output and prices of each type of cloth, in the light of foreseeable demand in both the international and the national market.

Below the drapers, but not as far below as the drapers would have liked, were three guilds of specialized craftsmen whose productivity and earning capacity were increased by heavy or elaborate tools: the dyers above all, then the fullers, and lastly the shearers. (Indeed, in some English towns the dyers played the leading role which elsewhere fell to the drapers.) A dyer who owned his vats and used expensive dyes rendered essential services to several drapers at one time and could be bullied by none; a fuller was in a similar position if he had a mill, but the peripheral location of the mill on a suburban river might limit his participation in town life; a shearer depended on his manual skill as much as on the moderate investment represented by his tools. This partly explains why the "blue nails" (dyers) played a prominent role in the popular revolution of the early fourteenth century, but the shearers remained in the background and the fullers bunched together with the weavers in earlier revolts that ended in failure.

Yet the weavers formed the indispensable core of the profession, were skilled workers using special tools, and eventually obtained official recognition for their guilds. With unconscious irony a twelfth century writer called them "knights on their feet who, by leaning on their stirrups (the pedals of the loom) relentlessly urge on their sober steeds." Sober is a fitting expression: by riding the pedal loom from eight to thirteen hours a day (the work day went from sunrise to sunset), a weaver could make a tolerably good living and scrape together some savings, but an illness or a temporary business recession could force him to run into debt or sell his tools, thus mortgaging his future at the hands of the money lender or the draper, who often were the same person. To the daring weaver, emigration might offer a remedy, although it was generally forbidden by town statutes; the rise of the industry in thirteenth-century Italy owed no little to a handful of Flemish immigrants. Note that the normal yearly production of a loom did not exceed thirty pieces of cloth.

Still below the weavers, but not quite at the bottom of the industrial pyramid, were such specialists as the combers and the carders, to whose modest skills and light tools the entrepreneurs paid some respect. At Douai in 1229, for instance, it was decreed that carders might request the town government to order an increase in their wages, provided the cost of living and market conditions permitted it. The town government, however, was in the hands of the drapers, one of whom, Jean Boinebroke, from an inquest into his estate after his death appears to have been one of the most wicked exploiters and usurers that has ever lived.

At the very bottom of the woollen industry was a depressed crowd of unskilled men and women who attended to such tasks as threshing and washing wool, spinning and warping, and had no chance to leave their hovels in town or in the suburban area except when they did domestic chores at the home of the entrepreneur. If the preindustrial rise did not revert to slavery or force workers into factories, it made more than a beginning in creating a proletariate and building a slum section. There is not much comfort in pointing out that extreme poverty in the rural areas could sink still lower.

GUILD BALANCE AND
PREINDUSTRIAL RISE
IN OTHER FIELDS

We cannot undertake in a few pages to explore one by one the other crafts that were affected to some degree by the medieval preindustrial rise; most of them, moreover, have bequeathed us fewer documents, or the documents have been less thoroughly studied. Without leaving the textile crafts, let us recall that silk cloth production in Italy was not far below woollen production in value if not in volume. Lucca, the principal center ever since the tenth century, lost her unchallenged primacy in the late thirteenth, when disgruntled craftsmen exported their talents and brought the throwing mill to Bologna and other cities; but she kept ahead of her competitors thanks to her unbroken tradition of superior artistic design and technical flawlessness. Again, the production of linen for garments, underwear, and bedding may have been larger than that of woollen; some fabrics were cheap but the best grades were exported to faraway places, even to China where no European woollens could be profitably shipped. Champagne and, to a lesser degree, the Swiss and German Rhineland were the most thriving centers of the craft, which was scattered all over northern Europe from the Low Countries to Russia, and to some extent in Spain, Italy, and Greece as well. Cotton textiles were chiefly for poorer customers; production depended less on specialized craftsmen than on religious orders, women, and country people who spun and wove as a side activity when their ordinary work slackened. Cheap labor and broad market opportunities, however, attracted many great merchants of northern and central Italy as early as the twelfth century to build up the production of fabrics of mixed cotton and wool (fustians or *mezzalani*). Around 1200 a piece of fustian sold for about one twentieth of the price of a piece of the best woollen; on this basis it was possible for a few entrepreneurs to give impulsion to a putting-out industry that came close to that of the English textile business on the eve of the Industrial Revolution.

The most remarkable manifestations of industrial entrepreneurship, however, occurred not in the textile crafts but in a mining, chemical, and commercial line of business partly related to them: alum. This double sulphate of aluminum and potassium, in a more or less pure form, found in the medieval processes almost as ubiquitous applications as those of sulphuric acid in modern industry. The most important uses were as a hardener in tanning (not a highly mechanized craft, although it eventually employed water mills, but one that served virtually every man), and as a color fastener in dyeing. Mineral deposits were very numerous around the Mediterranean and not rare elsewhere, but qualities varied considerably from one quarry to another, and affected the value of dyed materials. The fact that around 1300 alum from Volcano and Lipari (two small islands near Sicily), a good but not superior grade, was warmly recommended in England, merely accepted in Flanders, and strongly forbidden in Italy may help explain why England lost her supremacy to Flanders, and why Flanders could not prevent the Florentines from reexporting at great profit Flemish cloth dyed and finished in Florence. The best method of production was fairly simple, but time consuming: first calcination of the hewn material, then repeated leaching, then boiling, then slow crystallization in a vat; the purest and most valuable crystals emerged on top of the vat, the bottom yielded only inferior debris. A bulky material, alum was transported cheaply only by sea, preferably as ballast. Obviously the returns of producing and selling it would be maximized if the same entrepreneur owned a large quarry, processed the mineral in large vats, carried it in large ships, and controlled a large share of the market. Such an entrepreneurial paradise was conceived and welded together by the extraordinary ability and energy of a thirteenth-century Genoese merchant, Benedetto Zaccaria.

The activities of Zaccaria defy summary description. A member of the upper merchant class in his city, he earned money and renown as a naval commander at the service of the Byzantine Empire, of his own city, and of the kings of Castile and France. Beside winning battles under various flags he wrote in French a plan for the blockade of England, carried out delicate diplomatic missions, and was at different moments a pirate in the Aegean sea, a crusader in Syria, the governor of an Andalusian seaport, and the ruler of a Greek island. Between the Crimean peninsula and the Flemish shore there was scarcely a port that was never visited by one or many of the ships he personally owned, and scarcely a line of Genoese or Mediterranean business that he passed by. Let us consider only the moves that built his alum empire.

Zaccaria was a young but experienced trader in wool, cloth, and color dyes when he noticed a huge, clean deposit of alumite at a short distance from the good seaport of Phocaea, in Asia Minor. In 1274, he took advantage of a mission to the Byzantine court to obtain as a fief the whole region in return for naval assistance. There was only one quarry, also in Asia Minor, that yielded still better minerals; by political maneuvering Zaccaria blocked temporarily its exports, then by commercial bidding gained a share in them. Meanwhile he and his closest collaborators equipped the alum refineries near Phocaea with enormous vats, and protected them with a fortress on the land side and with cruising ships on the sea side. Italian technicians and artisans, and even a physician, joined the crews of sweated Greek laborers; fifty years after the opening of the works, a new agglomeration of about 3,000 inhabitants had grown to the south of the older seaport. The ships of Zaccaria took turns in transporting ever heavier alum cargoes to all destinations on the Mediterranean; they had on board weapons and soldiers in sufficient numbers to withstand an attack, and in some cases they also were covered by maritime insurance contracts. So long as northern Europe had to be reached by overland routes alum could not easily bear the cost of transportation to the main textile centers of England and Belgium; no wonder that ships belonging to the Zaccaria family were among the first mentioned as plying the direct sea route from the Mediterranean to England, as early as 1278. Twenty years later, a son of Zaccaria was sending alum ships to Bruges, while Zaccaria himself was helping the French king in his war against Flemish rebels. The naval campaign, however, was interrupted by a very medieval incident: Zaccaria heard that a group of male and female crusaders was preparing to sail from Genoa, and dropped everything in order to join them. Actually there was no crusade, and Zaccaria died not much later (1307 or 1308), but his descendants kept the alum industry and trade going. Around 1330 the annual production of Phocaea was estimated at almost 700 tons of refined alum, for an aggregate value of more than 50,000 Genoese pounds—

a modest amount in modern perspective, but an enormous sum for a single medieval entrepreneur. (Total alum production was of course much larger, but nowhere else controlled by a single man; three other mines in Asia Minor, for instance, had a combined output of about 1,800 tons).

The balanced, almost placid development of the decentralized building crafts forms a striking contrast with the sharp preindustrial rise of Zaccaria's concentrated alum business. On the basis of modern experience, some historians have postulated great booms of real estate and housing values as the inevitable consequence of medieval urbanization and economic growth. Such views, however, have so far found little confirmation in empirically collected data. New houses went up all the time, both to cope with demographic expansion and to keep up with rising expectations of comfort; but we do not hear of master masons or carpenters trying to grow rich by transforming their small scale operations into a mechanized integrated, chain-producing industry, or of merchant entrepreneurs financing and organizing a speculative contractors' trade. Random research on this still insufficiently explored subject suggests that masons' and carpenters' earnings left almost no margin for productive investment, and that merchants regarded houses as a conservative and prestige-giving investment but not a very profitable one. A study of rents paid for certain houses and shops in the commercial heart of Florence over a 52-year period that included the sharpest turns in both the economic and the demographic trends shows that the rents reacted to the changing conjuncture very moderately if at all. Perhaps the distances within a town were still too small to make a central location particularly desirable, and the frequent enlargements of city walls made it easy to prolong any crowded street into inexpensive suburban space.

No doubt there was more to medieval building than ordinary houses. Cathedrals, castles, town walls, bridges, and other monumental structures required an abnormally strenuous, concentrated, and prolonged effort. They could easily have stimulated industrial growth if they had been intended to yield unrestricted profit to the architects, the contractors, and the large crews of skilled and unskilled laborers who worked wonders with highly ingenious, yet altogether simple, methods and tools. (The basic tools were indeed so simple that a substantial proportion of the craftsmen assembled for such ambitious enterprises came from regional or international "lodges" of freemasons who were ever ready to pack up and move wherever an extraordinary need for help persuaded authorities to disregard any monopolistic claim of the local guilds.) In the Middle Ages as in antiquity, the greatest architectural commitments did not aim primarily at economic profit but at otherworldly or worldly security and glory, usually mixed with aesthetic gratification. The financing came from ecclesiastic, seigniorial, or communal funds, sometimes supplemented by more or less voluntary contributions from the broader public. They were sparingly administered by the promoters themselves or their representatives, who dealt out to the builders rather modest salaries and wages or, at most, conservatively calculated lump sums "for the task."

From a strictly economic point of view, we might note once again that cathedrals and castles took from the builders and from society as a whole much more than they paid back in terms of material welfare; bridges and other public works not only exacted smaller sacrifices, but also contributed more directly to economic growth. There are strong reasons to believe that in the thirteenth century the construction of Europe's tallest Gothic church crippled the development of Beauvais, hitherto a promising center of the textile industry, whereas the construction of a daring bridge near the Gotthard Pass hastened the transformation of southern Switzerland from a dead end of Germany into a live threshold of Italy. Man, however, lives not by bread alone. Let us not apply to cathedrals and bridges the invidious distinction that Frontinus made between the valuable Roman aqueducts and "the idle Pyramids or the famous but useless works of the Greeks." Let us consider, too, that the status of medieval builders represented great progress over the wretched condition of the slaves who built the Pyramids and the forced laborers who built the aqueducts.

Progress in mining and metallurgy was conditioned by conflicting pressures, which can be mentioned but briefly. The Commercial Revolution was by no means as dependent on metals as the Industrial Revolution. Wood, earthenware, and glassware rendered most of the services we now expect of nonprecious metals, which were then used only where extraordinary sharpness, sturdiness, or watertightness were indispensable. Precious metals were still the mainstay of monetary circulation and tantalized bullionist sovereigns and unproductive hoarders, but instruments of credit reduced their importance in the more developed countries. Every stage of production, from extracting the ore to delivering a finished artifact, demanded slow and painstaking manual work. No doubt economic and social conditions varied from one stage to another: the heavy toil of the miner was far less remunerative than the refined work of the goldsmith or the swordmaker, and there was at least a shade of difference between a maker of horseshoes and a maker of spurs. Small enterprise, however, was the common denominator. Rich or poor, virtually all members of the large and ramified family of smiths showed their predilection for the not too crowded workshop and the urban craft guild. A more rustic tradition, deriving from that of manorial agriculture, prevailed in the communities of miners and smelters of the mountainous, wooded recesses where most mines lay. Each family cultivated its share of the seam, but the methods in making pits, lifting ores, and smelting metals, as well as the hours of work and the division of profits were determined collectively by representatives of the miners and, usually, those of the prince or landowner who claimed part of the products as the lord of the soil. To a still greater degree than craft guilds, the customs of the miners (of which the earliest extant codification goes back to Trento in Northern Italy, 1185, and the largest body was issued in the Bohemian kingdom, 1249 and 1300) aimed at stability and equality at the price of mediocrity. They made mining a more decent occupation than it was in antiquity, when working in the mines was one of the worst penalties inflicted on criminals, but they provided no incentive for commercial investment and entrepreneurship.

Now let us look at the other side of the coin. Even though the demand for metals increased less than that for textiles, it certainly grew. We have mentioned the widespread adoption of iron and steel parts for agricultural tools; excellent blades and armor were the pride of the medieval knight, pikes and lances the typical weapon of yeomen and townspeople; few were the houses where some metal cauldrons did not strengthen the battery of breakable pots. The perennial hunger for silver, that lies behind so many governmental and private decisions, could not be merely an effect of greed, insecurity, or unfavorable balances of payment, but corresponded to a real need. Gold coinage, gradually introduced to almost every part of western Europe between the mid-thirteenth and the mid-fourteenth centuries, stimulated the quest for gold without diminishing that for silver. Again, miners were not just another subspecies of plain country workers; German miners, in particular, were reputed and welcomed throughout central and eastern Europe for their uncommon skills.

One could describe the history of mining in those regions as a series of sensational strikes and rushes, sometimes resulting from careful prospecting, more often incidental to forest clearing and frontier movement. As early as the tenth century the discovery of copper- and silver-bearing lead ores in the primeval woodlands of central Germany determined the growth of nearby Goslar from insignificant hamlet to capital of the Empire. Similar strikes in the following centuries led to the development of such thriving miners' towns as Freiberg in Saxony, Jihlava (Iglau) and Kutna Hora (Kuttenberg) in the Bohemian kingdom, Stora Kopparsberg in Sweden, and still other self-governing municipalities which brought a whiff of the Commercial Revolution to hitherto underdeveloped areas. But mining and metallurgy also gained new momentum in districts where they had been practiced in antiquity and almost abandoned in the barbarian age. The tin mines of Cornwall and Devon, exploited ever since prehistory, attained their peak in the thirteenth century, with a production of about 700 tons in one year; but they were in the periphery of economic development, and a Florentine company of merchant bankers that acquired an interest in them found the traditional methods and tools of the miners too inefficient for profit. Much greater profits were obtained from the iron mines of the island of Elba, of Etruscan and Roman fame; they were close to the main centers of Italian trade and became the bone of contention between Pisans and Genoese. The high quality iron of the Basque mountains was separated from its northern markets by the stormy bay of Biscay; the solution of the problem entailed progress in another field, that of steering. Good iron provided solid hinges for a central rudder, which had certain advantages over the lateral rudders previously used. We hear of the new rudder as a Basque specialty before 1300, and the same instrument that first helped Iberian iron-laden ships at a later time was to accompany Iberian caravels on the routes to the eastern and western Indies.

Two problems limited the growth of mining and metallurgy: the heavy consumption of fuel and the high cost of nonmechanized labor. Neither was fully solved during the Commercial Revolution, and this kept production down; the maximum figure we have just quoted for tin is not out of line with the approximately 4,500 tons of Basque iron exported in 1293. There were, however, important innovations, most particularly in the use of water and wind power. At various times in the thirteenth and early fourteenth centuries, modified types of the water mill were adopted here and there for driving forge-bellows, for activating heavy trip-hammers, for crushing ore, and for draining water from the deeper pits. Inventiveness was also displayed in the design of hearths, ovens, and furnaces. Remarkably, the blast furnace, which was the most significant step towards modern metallurgy, came as a byproduct of religion: it was first adopted in the twelfth century for casting huge church bells. Not much later, casting was also applied to making statues and household objects; but the process did not attract much capital and attention before the last years of the Commercial Revolution, when it was employed for the murderous purpose of making guns. Men in general, and governments in particular, seem to be readier to spend for death than to invest in life.

The shotgun wedding of metal and powder, however, could not have as decisive effects as a humbler mating of metal and coal. So long as wood remained virtually the only industrial fuel, mining and metallurgy were bound to consume far greater amounts than they replaced in more efficient tools and machines. No doubt wood was readily available wherever a new mine was opened in a forest clearing, but the very success of the mine burned it up at a dangerous pace. A net gain was possible only if coal was used as fuel, but its ugly color and bad smell discouraged potential users. Deforestation, and the presence of surface coal, by the thirteenth century got the better of consumers' resistance at Newcastle in England and at Liége in Belgium; but there was no great breakthrough, for Newcastle was not close to the best iron mines, and the best coal seams at

Liége were found right under the urban soil. The gains of coal-and-steel industry and the griefs of industrial pollution did not really get going before the Industrial Revolution of the eighteenth century.

Of the other medieval crafts that had potential for growth we shall mention only two that made some progress beyond the normal structure of guilds. Glass making in its most famous medieval manifestation, Gothic "stained" (or, more properly, painted) windows, was enmeshed in the same restraints that prevented cathedral builders from becoming preindustrial entrepreneurs. The larger market of ordinary houses did not take promptly to glass windows, which could not be produced cheaply by the normal process of blowing. Hollow vessels, however, were made as rapidly and cheaply as the market would bear; the best qualities fetched high prices; Venice maintained throughout the Middle Ages a strong edge over all competitors—and, incidentally, was the first to exploit industrially the scientific discovery of eyeglasses, as early as 1300. The glass industry, however, presented the same inconveniences as coal metallurgy: the furnaces were a fire hazard and gave out malodorous smoke. Hence the government obliged all glassmakers of the city to move to the suburban island of Murano. Togetherness, constant government supervision, and the close relations of the master craftsmen with the merchant entrepreneurs who exported the Venetian specialty oversea and overland, lent the Murano guilds of glassmakers some characteristics of an integrated industry and trade, but did not lead to an organization as tightly knit as that of the textile guilds.

A much larger potential for profitable entrepreneurship existed in the production and commerce of salt, whether from coastal lagoons and ponds or from rocks. The process by evaporation, however, was so simple, and salt-ponds so widespread, that it was difficult to bring them under unified control over large areas, although merchants from cities as far apart as Venice and Lübeck endeavored to do it. Salt mines were not as dispersed, and merchants could fairly easily persuade a government or a landowner to farm out to them the right of exploiting individual mines. Such was notably the case of the enormous mines of Wielicka, near Cracow, which were farmed first by German entrepreneurs, then by Genoese merchants; but a farmer's hold was revokable at the expiration of a contract and did not include feudal rights or any political or military power. We encounter a good number of successful businessmen in the salt industry and trade, but never a figure that may be compared to Zaccaria, the king of alum.

6

The Response of the Agricultural Society

DYNAMISM AND INERTIA IN THE AGRICULTURAL WORLD

To close our survey of economic growth and commercialization we have to take another look at the world of cathedrals, castles, and country people. For all the expansion of trade and crafts, agriculture (with such related activities as herding and lumbering) continued throughout and beyond the Middle Ages to be the main occupation or source of income and power for the overwhelming majority of the European population.

This is hardly surprising: the shifting of the occupational balance from mainly agricultural to mainly nonagricultural is a very recent phenomenon. As late as the mid-nineteenth century, with the Industrial Revolution well on its way, no large nation in Europe except England had disengaged more than half of its population from agricultural pursuits, and if we lumped together the population of the whole world today we would, no doubt, find that agriculture still is the prevalent occupation or source of income and power. Any attempt at calculating proportions in the Middle Ages would produce no more than guesses, but certainly agriculture loomed still larger at that time, with the Commercial Revolution well advanced but industrialization barely sketched. Although independent merchant republics by the thirteenth century controlled nearly all of northern and central Italy, and more or less autonomous urban communities pockmarked all of the other regions, most of the European surface was still in the shade of agrarian monarchies and fiefs. Again, although the organization of the church was traditionally hinged on cities, and although two town-based regular orders (the Franciscans and the Dominicans) in the thirteenth century had challenged the supremacy of land-based monasticism, agrarian interests and ways of thinking still were paramount in ecclesiastic circles. Indeed, agriculture had bridge-heads in every town: there were peasants living within the walls of the smaller ones, representatives of the king or territorial lord in all but the entirely independent cities, and religious institutions and powerful families living on income from country estates even in the Italian business capitals.

By its sheer mass and power, the agricultural society offered to the penetration of the Commercial Revolution both the widest opportunities and the strongest resistance. The former are obvious: though per capita consumption and production were higher in the cities, the aggregate production and consumption power of the countryside were incomparably greater, potentially at least. Still we must not forget the resistance. It partly stemmed from the instinctive antipathy of country people towards city people, a cleavage that has always existed and manages to survive in our highly industrialized, urbanized world. In the Middle Ages the antagonism was first deepened by the hostility of tough barbarian conquerors against soft Roman townsmen, then almost institutional-ized by the feudal notion of a tripartite society of noblemen, clergy-men, and peasants (with no recognized role for traders), and lastly exasperated by the resentment of conservative, slow-moving lords and farmers against pushy and revolutionary burghers. The Church, too, in spite of the efforts of Aquinas and a few other thinkers to reach a more equitable appreciation of the functions and needs of merchants, was unable to overcome the strictures of its own old-fashioned economic theories, formed in agrarian surroundings and hardened by Greco-Roman biases against trade. Not only did it include in the same condemnation usury proper and what we would call commercial interest, but it picked up the popular as-sumption that most merchants must be greedy exploiters and cheats. In turn the merchants normally charged interest, resented the pride of the lords and ridiculed the coarseness of the peasants (and here they rejoined the lords, who ordinarily held in contempt all laborers, including those who fed them). We cannot linger on these and other psychological disagreements in an economic essay, but we must note their unfavorable impact on collaboration between agriculturists and traders.

Mutual dislike, however, could not hinder profitable business relations as seriously as did the fact that agriculturists and traders marched to the beat of different drummers. The contrast in its extreme manifestations is best illustrated by a comparison between certain manorial obligations based on custom "existing from time immemorial" and certain commercial contracts dated not only by the day but even by the canonical hour (matins, prime, tierce, sext, nones, vespers, complin). Again, in Italian thirteenth-century cities literacy is an absolute requirement for merchants and craftsmen, but in a good many rural districts it is unheard of among peasants, abnormal among lay lords, and not to be taken for granted among lower clergymen. Merchants travel constantly and bring back useful economic information, but knights move only for war or pilgrimage and carry in their baggage too much complacency and xenophobia to leave room for learning; as for the peasants, they may take a few hints from their neighbors or export skills of their own to colonization lands, but they are usually too unlearned or too poor to engineer major changes. Scholars and high clergymen are more apt to travel with an open mind, but religious, philosophical, or political interests more often than not engross their attention and prevent their acquisitive instincts from engendering practical schemes for profit. Indeed, profit for profit's sake is a typically mercantile aspiration; preachers call it a sin. Not profit but "subsistence," calculated in proportion to status, is the acknowledged goal of the agrarian society. An ordinary English peasant may have to be content with dark bread and ale, whose prices are actually regulated by the king, whereas a monarch needs oversize subsistence; but even the king of France is expected to live off "his property," that is, the produce of his landed estates meagerly augmented by petty dues in cash, and only special emergencies entitle him to ask for extraordinary "aid."

These generalizations must of course be strongly qualified. To a still greater extent than trade, agriculture varies almost incredibly from one place or time to another. The difference between city and country dwindles to a minimum in the thickly settled parts of Italy and Belgium; and even those internal provinces of northern and eastern Europe that are least accessible to the main currents of trade do not forever stand still. Literacy and elementary accounting begin to find favor among members of the landed elite, at first chiefly as intellectual pastimes or legal and political equipment, but soon after as economic tools; the progress is best visible in the comparatively well-preserved manorial records of England. Powerful monastic orders gradually raise their expectations from enlarged subsistence to a frank pursuit of gain; the most conspicuous example is offered by the almost ubiquitous Cistercians, originally dedicated to personal toil on the land, then entrenched at the head of a network of "granges" where serfs and hired dependents carry out tillage or sheep-breeding with rational organization and methods. Nevertheless, we must keep in mind that subsistence needs were the prime motor of agricultural progress before the Commercial Revolution got going, and direct consumption continued thereafter to play a fundamental role in the economic life of the country. Population growth drove nobles, farmers, and peasants to look for new land and improved techniques: more land and improved techniques in turn supported further population growth. The chain reaction may be quickened by the input of commercial capital and initiative, but does not absolutely need it. Before we consider the commercial components of agricultural development, let us assess as best we can, on the basis of the spotty and hence disputable evidence we now have in hand, the elementary ingredients.

So far as we can tell, the rural population continued to grow throughout Europe until the Great Plague of 1346–48, and in some places (especially in eastern Europe) resumed its growth for a number of years after that crisis. It is probable that by the thirteenth century, if not earlier, accelerated urbanization caused the country to gain proportionately less than the cities. Nevertheless, the absolute size of the agricultural population was large enough to take urbanization in its stride without slowing down considerably its absolute natural increase. Again, the famine of 1315–17 had serious effects, but it was followed by many excellent harvests in the period 1325–45, in some parts of England at least; its repercussions can hardly have lingered thirty years to deliver the undernourished survivors and their children to the Great Plague, as has been sometimes claimed. Any increase in the incidence of birth control, about which we know virtually nothing except that it was practiced, may have affected the population curve more substantially; for only a very high birth rate could insure continuous demographic growth while the average expectation of life at birth, again in England, was about one half that of today: between thirty and thirty-five years according to the best estimates. (This in turn was better than the ancient Roman average of about twenty-five years, almost equal to China's average in 1946, and not much worse than the English average of barely above forty years in 1838–54.)

The tentative demographic profile we have thus traced agrees with available information on the expansion of cultivated areas, which went on, as a whole, unabated up to the mid-thirteenth century or shortly after and did not come anywhere to a full stop before the mid-fourteenth. The widest development opportunities continued to be found in the east and north central plains, where professional colonization entrepreneurs (*locatores*, sometimes designated by the prestigious title of *magistri indaginis*, "searchmasters") often assisted German, Slav, and Magyar princes and prelates in the gigantic task of filling the country with new farming settlements and adding strength and efficiency to older ones. We know very little about personalities and individual achievements, but the basic problems and strategy emerge clearly from twelfth and thirteenth century charters. The entrepreneur had to secure a concession and plan the layout of the future village according to the best economic and military considerations. He had to advertise in the more crowded countries to the west the advantages of receiving sizable plots of fertile land under convenient conditions of tenure; in the early period Flemish and Westphalian farmers responded eagerly, but increasing competition with urban labor markets made recruitment harder in spite of the continuing population pressure. Above all, the *locator* arranged for the transportation of the immigrants, supported them until the first harvest, prepared temporary shelter in enclosed camps, built churches, mills, and other utilities.

In return for this, he normally received from the overlord a package of rights and privileges resembling those of a vassal: part of the land as his free share, rents and dues from such public conveniences as bakeries, fisheries, inns, and mills, and the hereditary charge of administrator and judge of the new settlement. Whatever the original status of the agricultural promoters (there were noblemen, farmers, and townsmen), their economic role was not much unlike that of the merchant promoters we have met in the industrial field: they gathered capital, invested it at considerable risk, and contributed their technical competence and experience to the success of the enterprise.

There was successful expansion at many other places—not only in peripheral areas such as the subpolar forests of northern Scandinavia and Russia or in the war-torn borderland between Christian and Muslim Iberia, but also in smaller underpopulated pockets such as the swampy "fenlands" of England and the broken coasts of western Corsica—but by the mid-thirteenth century most of the better land in western and southern Europe was either thickly settled or fenced off as hunting, fishing, or grazing reserves. When, around 1300, we find that in certain districts of Normandy, Lincolnshire, or the Tuscan highlands the population was as large as today or even larger, we must conclude that some of the cultivated land was marginal and some was overcropped. It is not sure, however, that Europe as a whole had overstepped what then were the optimum limits of intensive agriculture: evidence is too scattered and sometimes inconsistent to warrant generalizations; moreover, optimum limits ought to be calculated with reference to the normal expectations of the times. In other terms, lords and peasants were accustomed to abysmally lower rewards in subsistence and surplus than modern agriculturists take for granted for the same amount of land and labor; so long as those rewards were obtainable, they would not feel that they had transgressed the law of diminishing returns.

We have pointed out at the beginning that progress in medieval agriculture depended to some extent on technological advances, but to a larger extent on the expansion of the cultivated area; the latter increased total production, but only the former could boost per capita production. Under these circumstances, it seems unfortunate that technological advances tended to slow down at the same time as the land still available for expansion shrank. Nearly all of the basic inventions and improvements in medieval agriculture, from the wheeled plough to the first experiments in three-course rotation of crops, can be traced back to the initial stage of expansion or earlier. To the later period we must ascribe a good number of minor improvements, but only two major ones: the introduction of the windmill and the addition to the plough of mould-boards which turned over the soil at greater depth. In agriculture the main technological contribution of the twelfth and thirteenth centuries was not a continuing flow of fresh innovations and more fruitful practices as in commerce and industry, but the slow propagation of earlier ones. This was undoubtedly an important achievement, for new machines and methods had in every instance to be adjusted to the particular ecology and needs of the place; the fact remains, however, that the average yield of cereals only doubled between the tenth century and the fourteenth, whereas commercial profits and industrial production grew at a much higher rate.

THE COMMERCIAL
COMPONENTS OF
AGRICULTURAL GROWTH

When we compare the steady but slow progress of self-centered agriculture with the accelerated gains brought about by commercialization, we are reminded of Daniel Defoe's imaginative comparison in his *Complete English Tradesman* (1726), published shortly before the take-off of the Industrial Revolution: "An estate's a pond, but trade's a spring: the first, if it keeps full, and the water wholesome, by the ordinary supplies and drains from the neighboring grounds, it is well, and it is all that is expected; but the other is an inexhausted current, which not only fills the pond, and keeps it full, but it is continually running over, and fills all the lower ponds and places about it." In the Middle Ages already, the impact of trade spurred certain sectors of the agricultural world to faster changes than those determined only or primarily by subsistence needs. Reactions, however, varied sharply from one country to another, from one social group to another, from one generation to another; we can briefly describe the main directions of change, but we shall not undertake to follow in detail the amount of progress accomplished in each region at every moment.

Probably the most widespread and obvious change was the general replacement of payments and tributes in kind (that is, in goods and services) by payments and tributes in cash or credit. This is what old-fashioned books used to call "the rise of money economy" as opposed to an earlier stage of "natural economy" or "closed economy." We now realize, however, that at no time in the Middle Ages was the European economy so introvert that every community lived exclusively on the natural products of its own soil and labor; there always were exchanges, no matter how small, and mediums of exchange to carry them out. Further, we no longer draw a firm line between money proper (that is, coins or written means of payment expressing a value in coin, such as instruments of credit or banknotes) and other mediums such as grain, oxen, cigarettes, or any other goods or services that at a given time happen to be more universally accepted in payment (in economic terms, "more liquid"). The legendary King Midas, who transformed all he touched into gold, was unfit to live; there were times and places in the Middle Ages when coined gold and silver would not easily be exchanged for other goods and services, but oxen were a sufficiently liquid "money." Still, coins normally possess many advantages that make them more liquid; by using them to a larger extent, agriculture fitted more snugly into the context of commercialization. As for credit, the great lubricant of the Commercial Revolution, it also made progress in agricultural economy, but not as much as in trade, and with more mixed effects. Merchants usually borrowed at moderate interest rates, looked forward to considerable profits for their investments, and could cover themselves against excessive risks by such contracts as the sea loan, the *commenda* and, later, insurance. Agriculturists had little or no coverage against risks, expected no extraordinary profits, and often paid high interest charges.

Actually the agricultural society resorted to credit for consumption purposes more frequently than for investment and development. If a harvest failed, a consumption loan, no matter how usurious, might be the only means for an improvident or impecunious farmer to survive until the next harvest. Certain forms of agrarian credit offered him some protection against unpredictable variations of climate: by selling "grain on the stalk" (before it was harvested) for a predetermined price, no matter how cut down by the buyer, a farmer might happen to receive at once a larger sum than the crop would be worth at harvest time. Ordinarily, however, excessive borrowing would reduce not only a needy or reckless consumer but also an overambitious investor to destitution and expropriation. Yet if we disregard his personal plight, a transfer of land from prodigal or inefficient hands to a more rational management may be counted an economic gain. Some of the best run baronial and ecclesiastic estates were built up by foreclosed mortgages; conversely, a negligent baron or abbot quickly dispersed the accumulated acquisitions of his predecessors. Though the official doctrine of the Church disapproved of all forms of interest-bearing loans, the records bear witness to systematic despoliation of tenants and neighbors at the hand of church administrators; they needed not lend at especially high rates, but more often than not they displayed greater order and persistence than their lay counterparts. Merchants were masters of the lending game, but their familiarity with the cooperative methods of trade made them more open to agreements that would help the borrower as well as the lender. Especially in Italy and southern France, they favored contracts whereby they advanced to tenants seed, animals, and tools in return for an increased but not unreasonable share of the product (up to one half). No such arrangements were offered by the hated Italian and Jewish usurers who made their living in the smaller towns and villages of Europe by fleecing depressed or spendthrift agriculturists. Yet it is doubtful that they charged more than native usurers; and they might have been more lenient if they had been less exposed to confiscation, extortion, and excommunication.

If credit on the whole tended to impoverish and enslave the inhabitants of the country, cash had the opposite effect. It enabled both lords and peasants to shop for a greater variety of market goods and spurred them to increase their marketable production in order to procure more cash; further, it loosened all inherited personal attachments to a master, a community, and a routine. Since maximum "liquidity" brought some benefits to all parties, it met with little opposition in the regions that had long been accessible to the free and individualistic practices of urban milieus, and penetrated fairly easily even in the most secluded manorial communities. The lord eagerly commuted the reluctant and inefficient deliveries of commodities and labor owed by the villeins into fixed monetary dues, and used part of the proceeds to hire specialized seasonal help for a better exploitation of his demesne; sometimes he chose to put out to lease the demesne as well and live entirely on rents, with no further concern for the management of his land. The peasants took advantage of released time and dispensation from consignment of specific goods to orient their production towards an external, competitive market; sometimes they chose to supplement agricultural income by setting up rustic workshops or accepting such work as was put out by the urban crafts. Distinctions between serfdom and free tenancy became blurred as both entailed financial rather than personal obligation, and this accelerated the movement towards universal enfranchisment. By the mid-thirteenth century, serfdom had almost entirely disappeared in northern and central Italy; in France it was officially abolished on royal estates in the early fourteenth century and became exceptional in several regions on private domains; great patches of free peasantry emerged at about the same time in Switzerland, southern and western Germany, the Low Countries, and, somewhat later, in England. What is more, serfdom, like labor services and payments in kind, now tended to fade away quietly, no longer as a result of clashes between dependents and masters, but mainly because neither party regarded it as very helpful. The agrarian ideal of security based on permanent mutual obligations was slowly bending towards the commercial quest for opportunity based on temporary contractual agreements.

The influence of trade was more direct and powerful in promoting specialization. It did not seriously affect the general tendency of agriculturists to produce indiscriminately all the basic foodstuffs needed for their own maintenance, but it guided them in planning the production of surpluses. Preexisting local traditions were strengthened or weakened accordingly as soil quality, communications, labor conditions and skills favored or hindered a specific culture. In the early period of the Commercial Revolution, even the most unpromising districts strove to produce more cereals than they ordinarily consumed, if only to make sure that they would have enough on a bad year. By 1300, however, the Teutonic Knights were gaining partial control of the northern international market; their freshly developed lands were fertile; large rivers conveyed their crops from the flat hinterland to the Hansa ports; labor was cheap and everything was efficiently organized. On southern markets, Sicily, ancient Rome's granary, still played an important role thanks to its good maritime communications and the depressed standard of living of its peasants; Italian merchants, however, were increasingly relying on countries outside Catholic Europe, from southern Russia and the Balkans to Morocco, for supplementary imports. There were many minor exporters—Brandenburg, Suffolk, Ile-de-France, and many others—but some of the lands that would have been most suitable, including the Po valley and the Belgian plain, did not even take care of their own needs.

Not unlike cereals, wine was produced for local consumption wherever vines would grow, even in Gloucestershire where, according to the French chancellor of Henry II, one had better gulp it "with closed eyes and with tense jaws." The early period of the Commercial Revolution was marked by almost indiscriminate expansion: landlords granted plots and reduced dues to any tenant who planted new vineyards, sourly fermented juices were made palatable by the addition of honey and spices, and medieval containers were not tight enough to let age bring out the distinction between superior and inferior kinds. By the thirteenth century, however, the map of prized brands was taking shape, and certain districts (Auxerre, for instance), had converted all their soil to vineyards. The same provinces of France that are famous today gave the best and most widely exported dry wines; costly sweet wines were the specialty of Greece; Italian and Rhineland wines had regional fame rather than international celebrity. What mattered in every instance was not only the natural virtue of soil and climate, but also the proximity of waterways; for the weight of the barrels made overland transportation exceedingly expensive, and a barrel easily collapsed when carried over a bumpy road.

Though not a product of the soil, preserved fish cannot be omitted from the top triad of best-selling food crops. Scanian herring, as we have seen, was firmly in the lead, but international trade paid much attention to other fish, ranging from tough Icelandic stockfish to mellow caviar of the Black Sea. To a smaller extent, English bacon, Scandinavian butter, Iberian and Italian nuts, Cyprus sugar, and many other foodstuffs (too many for listing) had also become the object of specialized production and trade.

Industrial (or rather, "preindustrial") development also stimulated agricultural specialization. Wool, like grain and wine, had been and continued to be produced everywhere: the demand kept growing, and virtually no lord was too rich or peasant too poor to neglect the cash that sheep could raise for him. The lower French, Italian, and German grades were good enough for homespun or cheap and medium-priced commercial textiles. When the very best was desired, northern Europe called for English wool, and southern Europe for Spanish or African wool. Apparently English sheep were so scrawny that one of them gave at most one pound of wool; but there were perhaps as much as eight millions of them (two for every inhabitant of the kingdom), and the king, whose finances heavily depended on wool duties, pushed the product with foreign merchants while forbidding them to take out in cash their earnings from anything they sold or lent. This, and the generally acknowledged superiority of English wool, after the mid-thirteenth century, endangered the standing of Spanish and African wool in the Italian quality market. Perhaps in response to the challenge, the Castilian king in 1273 granted extraordinary privileges to the guilds of migratory sheep; Genoese merchants shortly after turned their attention to an African breed that was destined for a great future, the long-haired *merino*. Still it took more than two centuries before Castilian-bred merinos eclipsed all competitors; moreover, Spain paid a heavy price in the damage inflicted by sheep shuttling back and forth through miles of forest and cultivable land.

It would be long to run through the list of medieval industrial crops, even if we limited it to textile fibers and vegetable dyestuffs, which were as prominent among those crops as was cloth-making among industries. Let us consider only the two commonest dyes, sold by the ton rather than by the pound and ground by mills rather than by hand: red madder and blue woad. Both of them were cultivated almost ubiquitously, but in the course of the Commercial Revolution the production tended to concentrate in a few districts at a short distance from industrial regions. Madder root fetched higher prices, but it had to grow for two years before it was picked, and uprooting destroyed the plant. Woad leaves, on the contrary, were picked four or five times a year without harming the plant; or else the plant could be fitted into the rotation of cereal crops. It was sown in arable fields after grain had been harvested, picked before the next sowing of food crops, and the stalks without leaves were reused as fodder. Sooner or later any intelligent farmer was bound to realize that woad was more profitable than madder; by the fourteenth century a change in fashion, that made red-colored cloth less approved than blue-colored cloth in elegant circles, accelerated the shift and caused woad production to soar.

We cannot always tell what influence profit-minded merchants may have had in promoting changes in production and fashion, but a pervasive connection between commercial and agrarian initiative is clearly indicated in the Italian manuals of commercial practice that appear from the late thirteenth century on. They describe with almost incredible precision the quality, cost, size, and other characteristics of every commodity available at every seaport or distribution center where merchants and agriculturists met. They often tell what ways and means of transportation are cheaper and safer, what taxes and tolls one has to expect, when an item will be ready for delivery, and how abundant is the normal crop. One of the manuals shows us the agents of a Florentine company of merchant bankers making the rounds of Apulian villages where the best local cheeses are sold, and, a few pages further, other agents of the same company using a list of every Cistercian and Premonstratensian monastery of England where fine wool can be had.

Lay and ecclesiastic landowners often meet the merchants more than half-way. One example will suffice, that of Thierry d'Hireçon, a slightly younger contemporary of Benedetto Zaccaria (he died in 1328), who was Bishop of Arras and owner of several estates in northern France. Like Zaccaria, Thierry managed his business with the most advanced methods that the mature experience of the

Commercial Revolution had found. For ploughing and harrowing, the fundamental operations in the production of cereals, he employed domestic servants, who lived on the estate the whole year, and paid them both food and wages; for the smaller tasks he hired unattached farm hands, paying them by the day or the job, in cash or in kind, as seemed most convenient to him. He used iron tools and four-horse ploughs unstintingly, prepared the winter's sowing by four successive ploughings, and thus obtained such bumper yields for wheat as 8.7 to one in a recorded case, and 12.8 to one in another. The spring crop, in one of his estates, at least, consisted mainly of soil-enriching leguminous plants. Cereals sold best in the Flemish cities: the bishop shipped them directly by water to merchants of Ghent and Bruges, paying for transportation in one recorded instance about 17 per cent of the selling price. He also sold wood, by auction or retail sales, raised pigs for profit, and doubled in less than one year his original investment in a flock of sheep, which he had bought in fall when prices were lowest and resold at a more favorable moment after having taken and sold their wool.

No doubt Bishop Thierry was as outstanding among agriculturists as a Bonsignori or a Bardi among merchants. Arras, his see, was a thriving industrial and financial center in the midst of unusually fertile land. Still his discriminating management indicates a change of mentality that was no longer restricted to a few urbanized areas. If one compares the manual of agriculture of Pietro de Crescenzi, a Bolognese judge and landowner, with the approximately contemporary English manual of Walter of Henley (thirteenth century), one finds that the former is more sophisticated and aware of Roman agronomic theory, but the latter has practical experience and shrewdness enough to make the most of every chance for profit. And if Padua, Venice, and other Italian cities were first in providing mechanical clocks on public squares to remind people that time is money, a few English castles did not take long in following suit.

THE DARK SIDE OF
THE PICTURE

To go back where we started, let us remember that only a small fraction of the agrarian scene is clearly visible, mostly through documents written by and for the enterprising rich. Much of the rest is literally immersed in darkness, on which scholars have but recently begun to project the dim light of such auxiliary sciences as the study of pollens and the analysis of buried metals. And while it does not seem unwarranted to assume that by and large t' ɔ pattern of commercial development in the better-known leading cities resembled that of obscure ones, we cannot make the same assumption in regard to agricultural development; the country, it will never be said too often, is a poor conductor. Even in the restricted area for which information is available, we can and should notice conflicting drives.

We have pointed out that increasing commutation of payments in kind and labor services into monetary rents generally benefited both the lords and the peasants. All parts of this statement, however, need qualification. At one time or another, many lords discovered that the flat cash dues for which they had settled were whittled down by debasement of coinage and increased cost of living. Then they tried to reintroduce some form of alternative payment (either cash or commodities and labor, at their choice), or they imposed new contributions, no longer as landowners but as feudal governors of the land. The peasants, too, not always found it convenient to scrape together cash for rent by offering their produce and labor in an unpredictable open market, where the weak and the needy might be mercilessly exploited. Especially if their land was overcropped, burdened with debts, or exposed to enemy incursions, they would rather preserve or restore the ties of the traditional village community, where the lord carried most responsibilities in return for fixed labor services and prorated deliveries of goods. Personal freedom, a great step forward if it opened the door to expanding opportunities, became an undesirable burden if it entailed heavy additional liabilities. Significantly, the

French ordinance of 1315, which offered to the king's serfs enfranchisement in the lofty name of the "natural liberty of all men," added in the same breath that should anyone choose "to remain in the humiliation of serfdom," he would nevertheless be subject like the others to a new war tax imposed on free men.

Opportunity existed in agriculture as in commerce, but it was less accessible and, above all, less elastic. Not only were there many villages that remained out of reach of the Commercial Revolution, but every village depended on a delicate ecologic balance that was easily upset by progress. Demographic growth was generally a factor of economic development, but if the population of a specific locality grew too fast and the excess was not absorbed by urbanization and emigration, plots became too small for efficient cultivation, and no adequate provision was made for the livestock whose draft power, fleece or meat and, above all, whose manure were badly needed. If, on the contrary, too much space was allotted to sheep-raising or industrial crops, the community lost its primordial asset, the ability to feed itself. Protected seigniorial forests and ponds, the object of peasants' hatred, were no longer large and well distributed enough to neutralize the accumulative ravages of deforestation, soil erosion, and hydraulic disorder caused by countless generations of men and sheep. The small commercial farmer dreaded abnormally bad and abnormally good harvests almost equally: the former depleted granaries, the latter depressed prices. Liquid capital, generally scarce even among the largest landowners, was not always poured into productive investments such as the purchase of tools and livestock, but often spent for irrational acquisition of scattered additional land, or for those enormous banquets and celebrations that broke the monotony of country life. And even the best administrators miscalculated their chances: the extant accounts of estates seldom match the high yields optimistically suggested by manuals of agriculture, and some of them, especially after the mid-thirteenth century, show declines.

Can we reconstruct, on such localized evidence, a general trend? The disconnected texture of the agrarian landscape tended to isolate failure as much as success. Overcrowding and underpopulation, blight and bliss existed side by side. By the thirteenth century, as documents become more abundant, we catch glimpses of trim, thriving farmers' towns (in Tuscany, for instance) with communal administrators, judges and notaries, with artisans of all crafts, with stores full of city goods, and even with schools. We find affluent communities of herdsmen in the highest valleys of Switzerland, and we can identify a few rich peasants almost everywhere. On the other hand, poverty does not spare the high-born. There is the lord of Tintinnano near Siena, who begs the commune for money to buy a pair of sandals; there are the numerous children of the lower nobility, whose only hopes for decent living are a profitable marriage (sometimes with the daughter of a rich farmer) or military, religious, and bureaucratic employment with a higher lord. Towns offer hope to the ambitious and the uprooted; but a great many peasants are unable or unwilling to move, even if they have to live in more wretched circumstances than the lowest urban proletarians. They sleep in mud hovels or caves, which they sometimes share with chickens and other farm animals, own almost no furniture or linen, and can stretch the scarce food grown in their tiny plots only by working for miserable wages on other people's land. Still the worst degree of destitution in the thirteenth century does not seem as stark as that of many serf and slave peasants of the tenth; and increased distances between the very rich and the very poor are the normal result of ages of growth, including our own. All told, there is no reason to depart from the tentative diagnosis we suggested in regard to population growth, expansion of cultures and technological progress: continuing improvement throughout the age of the Commercial Revolution, with constant or increasing acceleration up to the mid-thirteenth century, but with a tendency towards a slackening pace in the last decades of that century and the first half of the fourteenth.

FROM ATTRITION TO CONTRACTION: THE REVOLUTION COMES TO A HALT

The retardation of agricultural development in the last hundred years before the Great Plague of 1346–48 had an attenuated parallel in a number of disturbances that affected commercial and craft development to some extent. Demography is the sector where the parallelism was closest: many towns seem to have slowed down or arrested their growth after 1250, and even Florence, after attaining her medieval peak around 1300, underwent a very slight population decrease. The adverse trend, however, was not so pronounced or generalized that it may not be explained by intensified birth control or various local causes. The other unfavorable occurrences were still more localized, or external to the main economic process: wars in France, in the Levant, and between or inside towns; taxation and forced loans connected with the wars; bank failures that did not, however, prevent the formation of new banks on the ruins of the old ones; declining profits in ordinary trade, but with lower risks; contractions in the Flemish woollen industry and the Lucchese silk industry that may have been offset by the expansion of younger textile centers; depletion of certain silver mines that was probably compensated by exploitation of other veins. It has been claimed that these and other attritions, combined with the retardation of agricultural growth, prepared the ground for the more serious blow of the Great Plague and its consequences. This is an attractive hypothesis, but we lack precise data to prove or disprove it.

At any rate, we must distinguish the strains of agriculture, which affect essential needs such as the nourishment of the cultivator and irreversible processes such as soil erosion, from the incidental setbacks that trade can take in its stride and sometimes turn into advantages. War brings dividends to the merchant and the maker of swords. Forced loans suggest to the businessmen in charge of municipal finances the gimmick which might have made the Roman Empire both solvent and popular if the emperors had thought of it: funded debt, that is, an advance of capital which does not have to be returned at any specified time but brings to the lenders a steady income from the proceeds of regular taxation. It was always possible for a merchant to diversify his investments according to his preferred ratio of risks and profits. Commercial and industrial competition produced both winners and losers, but the net result, in a world that was still too fragmented for international monopolies, cartels, and protectionisms to stifle initiative, was a continuous search for new methods, new routes and new markets.

Without going into further detail, let us point out that the very mechanism of economic growth generates at every step its own wear and tear, its jams and imbalances; but it also mends itself by re-sharpening its parts, removing or turning one obstacle after another, adding new tools and discovering fresh outlets. Indeed there are indications that, in Genoa at least and most probably at other places whose evidence has been less thoroughly studied, cycles of crest and trough like those that characterized the so-called "dynamic equilibrium" of a very long stretch of the Industrial Revolution were already at work in the thirteenth century and possibly in the twelfth as well. They caused temporary trouble and worry, but they did not deflect the upward direction of the secular trend.

Whatever the attrition, on the eve of the Great Plague the medieval merchant was seemingly bound for ever greater economic success. He had just added China to his backyard, insurance to his fences, many kinds of mills to his tool shed; he wore new glasses to verify his new double-entry books of accounting, and probably did not mind the new medicine some doctors were prescribing, "water of life," that is, distilled spirits. In his home town, he made the good and the bad weather, with a self-assurance, or indeed an arrogance his Greco-Roman predecessors would never have dreamed of, and his modern successors would not dare display. Quite cocky even abroad, when dealing with sovereigns who depended heavily on his economic or military cooperation, he spoke more softly to the great monarchs of the age. Still his actual power was transparent under the mantle of the most intractable king of the strongest European state, Philip the Fair of France (1285–1314): the sovereign who challenged both Pope Boniface VIII and King Edward I of England entrusted his tangled finances to a Florentine merchant (Musciatto Guidi) and his fledgling navy to a Genoese merchant (Benedetto Zaccaria).

No doubt there were many people who complained that alien moneylenders came "with nothing but a pen and an inkpot" to write down the advances made out to kings or peasants in the form of simple vouchers, and in return for such scribblings eventually carried off the material wealth of the land. But the merchants also wrote books in large number. It is no small token of their ascendancy in the thirteenth and early fourteenth century that the most widely copied and read book was that of Marco Polo, where practical information on markets interlards the romance of travel, and that the greatest poem of the entire Middle Ages was written by a registered if not very active member of the Florentine guild of spice-sellers, Dante Alighieri. The merchants also built town halls, arsenals, hospitals, and cathedrals. When the Great Plague struck, Siena had just begun work on an extension of her enchanting Duomo, so that it would outdo the cathedral of her neighbors and commercial rivals in Florence. Evidently the crash of the Bonsignori bank had not destroyed Siena's financial competitiveness. The Great Plague did: the majestic, unfinished remains of the "Duomo Nuovo" eloquently confirm the testimony of written records.

It is not our task to follow up the general crisis that brought the Commercial Revolution to a halt after 1348, and it would be impossible to examine in a few lines the debated problems of its origin, impact, limits, and duration. In the writer's opinion, the commercial attrition and agricultural saturation that preceded the crisis were not incurable. They might have been solved if they had not been compounded by three agents of secular depression. These may have been latent before 1346–48 but came to the fore in the second half of the thirteenth century: protracted and destructive wars in western Europe and the entire continent of Asia; a sudden return of periodically recurring, hemisphere-wide epidemics that went on for almost three hundred years; and a new pulsation of climate that made it harder for nature to repair the wounds inflicted by man. War, plague, climatic change: these had been the major disasters that broke the economy of the Roman Empire. Happily, the Commercial Revolution had built up economic strength and resilience far beyond the classic peak of golden mediocrity; hence the economy of medieval Europe declined somewhat, but did not fall.

Suggestions for Further Reading

I: GENERAL WORKS

The *Cambridge Economic History of Europe*, vols. I–III (1941–63; partially revised edition of vol. I, 1966), is the most comprehensive survey of the entire medieval period and altogether the best cooperative work on the subject. It includes essays by eminent masters, some of whom also were gifted writers. Too large and uneven for easy reading from cover to cover and not everywhere up to date, it remains nevertheless indispensable for consultation, methodology, and extensive bibliographic guidance. (Henceforth referred to as C.E.H.)

Three smaller volumes in the French collection *Nouvelle Clio* (Presses Universitaires) cover the same ground with less emphasis on facts and with useful suggestions of work to be done: R. Doehaerd, *Le haut moyen âge occidental, économies et sociétés* (Paris, 1971); L. Genicot, *Le XIIIe siècle européen* (1968); J. Heers, *L'Occident aux XIVe et XVe siècles, aspects économiques et sociaux* (1966).

The best one-volume cooperative history in English is the *Fontana Economic History of Europe*, I (Fontana, London, 1972), which brings up to date (in a sketchier way) the bibliography of C.E.H. and touches some problems inadequately examined in it, but in no way supersedes it. Another cooperative history (in German but with international collaboration), *Handbuch der europäische Sozial- und Wirtschaftsgeschichte*, is expected to appear soon (Ernst Kleist, Stuttgart). Of one-author, one-volume works the most detailed is probably that of G. Fourquin, *Histoire économique de l'Occident médiéval* (Presses Universitaires, Paris, 1969), a useful book, whereas R. Latouche's mediocre *The Origins of Medieval Economy* (Barnes and Noble, New York, 1961) hardly deserved an English translation. Lastly one may mention G. Hodgett, *A Social and Economic History of Medieval Europe* (Methuen, London, 1972), clear but elementary, and R.H. Bautier, *The Economic Development of Medieval Europe* (Thames and Hudson, London, 1971), more original, and sometimes controversial. Two short essays, not covering as fully the economy of the Middle Ages, also provide fresh insights: C. M. Cipolla, *Before the Industrial Revolution (1000–1700)* (Norton, New York, 1976), and J. Gimpel, *La révolution industrielle du moyen âge* (Seuil, Paris, 1975).

Of economic histories restricted to individual countries the following should be noted: ENGLAND, J. Clapham, *A Concise Economic History of Britain* up to 1700 (Cambridge University Press, 1949), somewhat outdated but readable and well balanced; M.M. Postan, *The Medieval Economy and Society, an Economic History of Britain, 1100–1500* (University of California Press, Berkeley, 1972), vigorously controversial. ITALY, G. Luzzatto, *An Economic History of Italy from the Fall of the Roman Empire to 1600* (Barnes and Noble, New York, 1961), somewhat outdated and very concise but excellent; and the essays of various authors, with an introduction of C.M. Cipolla, all in Italian, *Storia dell'economia italiana*, I (Boringhieri, Turin, 1959). FRANCE, not so much the old and mediocre *Histoire économique de la France*, I, by H. See and R. Schnerb (Colin, Paris, 1948), as the essays of various authors edited by R. Cameron, *Essays in French Economic History* (Irwin, Homewood, Ill., 1971). SPAIN, J. Vicens Vives, *An Economic History of Spain* (Princeton University Press, 1969), partly outdated but excellent. GERMANY, F. Lütge, *Deutsche Sozial- und Wirtschaftsgeschichte*, in *Enzyklopädie der Rechts- und Staatswissenschaft* (Berlin, 1960), competent, short, dull. NEAR EAST, the essays of various authors, edited by M.A. Cook, *Studies in the Economic History of the Middle East* (Oxford University Press, 1970).

While referring the readers to the works listed above for further bibliographic information, we should specifically mention two classic works that have lost nothing of their methodological value even though the information is dated and some of the hypotheses are no longer regarded as valid: H. Pirenne, *Histoire économique et sociale du Moyen Age* (2nd ed., partially revised by H. Van Werveke, Presses Universitaires, Paris, 1963), and M. Bloch, *Feudal Society* (University of Chicago Press, 1960). Though not on the same level, R.L. Reynolds, *Europe Emerges* (University of Wisconsin Press, Madison, 1961), contains stimulating suggestions. Lastly, my own *The Birth of Europe* (Evans-Lippincott, New York, 1967) develops more fully some of the concepts outlined in the present book.

II: PARTICULAR TOPICS AND PROBLEMS

The central methodological problem in economic history—combining the humanistic approach of history with the social science approach of economics—can be tackled in more than one way; see, for instance, the March 1971 issue of the *Journal of Economic History*, where scholars of different tendencies, generations, and preparations have reviewed past works and offered suggestions for the future. Unfortunately, however, what should be an enriching dialogue between historians trained in economic analysis and economists aware of historical structure is still hampered by mutual diffidence and inferiority complexes. The debate has lately centered on a badly-put question, whether quality or quantity is the prime raw material for study. They actually are two faces of the same coin: adjectives usually imply a quantitative assessment (we call "rich" a man who owns or earns

more than a certain amount), figures derive their significance from qualitative judgments ("five percent of the population was literate" explains
nothing unless we consider what was read, what was absorbed, and what
influence it had on the entire society). When it comes to medieval economic history, whose extant sources deliver very few and often unreliable
figures, with adjectives mostly reflecting the views of privileged individuals
or classes, economic historians need all the help of both general history
and general economics to draw a plausible though never definitive picture.

Man (with woman, of course) is the protagonist of history and the
measure of all things; but in medieval demography, prudence is the best
part of valor. Even the most erudite and technically sophisticated general
works, such as J. Russell, *British Medieval Population* (University of New
Mexico Press, Albuquerque, 1948) and R.J. Mols, *Introduction à la
démographie historique des villes d'Europe du XIVe au XVIIIe siècle*
(3 vols., Université de Louvain, 1954–6), are based on hazardous extrapola-
tions from fragmentary positive data. We do have precise information for
small stretches of time and space; for the rest, we must mainly rely on a
mass of impressions.

G. Duby, *Rural Economy and Country Life in the Medieval West* (University of South Carolina Press, Columbia, 1968), offers an excellent survey
of the history of agriculture from the Carolingian period to the end of the
Middle Ages, where analysis and synthesis, economic realities and historical ideologies are equally stressed; its bibliography is almost exhaustive.
His *Guerriers et Paysans, VIIe–XIIe siècles* (Gallimard, Paris, 1973) goes
farther back in time and broadens the picture to other aspects of economic
life. Less important, but still useful for its grasp of peasant customs, is
R. Grand and R. Delatouche, *L'Agriculture au Moyen Age* (De Boccard,
Paris, 1950). Those who prefer a strictly economic approach to a broadly
humanistic one may choose to read B.H. Slicher van Bath, *The Agrarian
History of Western Europe* (Arnold, London, 1963), a competent book,
sometimes beclouding the insufficiency of extant data under bold extra-
polations and sheer guesswork. On the other hand, E. Sereni, *Histoire du
paysage rural italien.* (Laterza, Bari, 1964), supplementing strictly economic information with an unusual wealth of pictorial and literary material, will be especially suggestive for some other readers.

No recent book is devoted to a general survey of the history of commerce, but chapters IV and V of C.E.H., II, and chapter II of C.E.H., III
(respectively by M.M. Postan, R.S. Lopez, and R. de Roover), give an
almost complete panorama if read consecutively. None of the later general
works on medieval economic history covers the ground or the bibliography
as thoroughly, though R. Roehl's chapter 3 in the *Fontana Economic
History* ("Patterns and Structure of Demand") provides interesting if
sketchy comments on one aspect not adequately dealt with in C.E.H., and
though bibliographies, of course, are more up to date in later works. On
the other hand, the general history of commerce plays an important part

in the best books of urban history. Leaving a few monographs on individual cities for the third section of this orientation, we mention here the following studies concerning whole regions or merchant classes: J. Le Goff, *Marchands et banquiers du Moyen Age* (Presses Universitaires, Paris, 1956); J. Lestocquoy, *Les villes de Flandre et d'Italie sous le gouvernement des patriciens* (Presses Universitaires, Paris, 1952); P. Dollinger, *The German Hansa* (London, 1970); A. Sapori, *Le marchand italien au Moyen Age* (Colin, Paris, 1952); D. Waley, *The Italian City-Republics* (McGraw-Hill, New York, 1969). General bibliography on medieval cities and comments on urban typology are in R.S. Lopez' paper, "The Crossroads within the Wall," included in O. Handlin and J. Burchard, ed., *The Historian and the City* (M.I.T. and Harvard University Presses, 1963).

There is no recent book on the general history of industry either, and C.E.H. deals in detail with only two branches, woolen cloth (by E. Carus-Wilson; good, but somewhat English-centered) and mining (by U. Nef; good, with some moralistic undertones); but Sylvia Thrupp's ch. 6 in the *Fontana History* provides an excellent if short survey, with an underdeveloped bibliographic list. A few monographs on individual crafts will be mentioned in the third section. Strictly connected with the subject is the good book of P. Wolff, *Histoire générale du travail*, I, part 1 (Nouvelle Librarie de France, Paris, 1961; the illustrations are an asset); so is S. Thrupp's chapter on guilds in C.E.H. III.

The history of techniques (both tools and methods) is an important part of all aspects of economic history; so is that of transportation. On hardware the largest but not everywhere the best surveys are the cooperative ones edited by C. Singer, *A History of Technology*, vols. II and III (Oxford University Press, 1956-7), and by M. Daumas, *Histoire générale des techniques*, vols. I and II (Paris, 1962-7); but one should not miss Lynn White's stimulating, if occasionally overenthusiastic, *Medieval Technology and Social Change* (Oxford University, 1962), and the spirited sketch of S. Lilley, *Men, Machines, and History* (London, 1948). On business law and methods the comments, texts, and bibliography of R.S. Lopez and I.W. Raymond, *Medieval Trade in the Mediterranean World* (Columbia University Press, New York, 1955) and the previously mentioned chapter of R. de Roover in C.E.H. III provide a virtually complete survey. Nothing of the kind exists for transportation, but the *Actes* of the Colloque International d'Histoire Maritime (M. Mollat, ed.; Paris, 1956ff.), plus the sketch of R.S. Lopez, "The Evolution of Land Transport in the Middle Ages," in *Past and Present* (1956) are of some help.

On the crucially important subjects of money, credit, and prices there is a plethora of monographs but no satisfactory general survey. C.M. Cipolla, *Money, Prices and Civilization in the Mediterranean World* (Princeton University Press, 1956) is a stimulating introduction to some aspects; further bibliography on monetary history can be found in R.S. Lopez, *Il ritorno all'oro nell'Occidente duecentesco* (Edizioni Scientifiche italiane,

Naples, 1955); on banking and credit several essays included in A. Sapori, *Studi di storia economica*, 3 vols. (Sansoni, Florence, 1955) are fundamental, but one can also use Sapori's popularization, *Merchants and Companies in Ancient Florence* (limited edition: La Fondiaria, Florence, 1955) and de Roover's *The Rise and Decline of the Medici Bank* (Harvard University Press, 1963, though the latter focusses on a later period.

Studies on the relations between church, state, and businessmen are innumerable and mostly restricted to specific aspects; some of them will be listed in the third section. Relations between economics and culture have been discussed mostly in short papers, such as H. Pirenne, "L'instruction des marchands au Moyen Age," *Annales d'Histoire Economique et Sociale*, I (1929), and, in the same magazine, R.S. Lopez, "Economie et architecture médiévale" (1952); the debate is still in progress.

III: MONOGRAPHIC WORKS

An adequate bibliography of monographs (both books and articles, some of which are as significant as some general books) would take up another volume, and duplicate the bibliographies of the works quoted in the first two sections. The small numbed listed hereafter is an arbitrary sampling, with preference given to studies at least partly in English or French.

(a) *Individual cities, regions, or social groups*

F.C. Lane, *Venice, a Maritime Republic* (Johns Hopkins University Press, Baltimore, 1973).

R.S. Lopez, *Su e giù per la storia di Genova* (Università di Genova, 1975).

D. Herlihy, *Pisa in the Early Renaissance* (Yale University Press, New Haven, 1958).

F. Schevill, *History of Florence* (Constable, London, revised 1961).

L. Martines, ed., *Violence and Civil Disorder in Italian Cities* (University of California Press, 1972).

E. Baratier and F. Reynaud, *Histoire du Commerce de Marseille*, II (Plon, Paris, 1951).

H. van Werveke, *Bruges et Anvers* (Brussels, 1944).

L. Genicot, *L'économie rurale namuroise au bas moyen âge* (Université de Louvain, 1943).

E. Le Roy Ladurie, *Les paysans du Languedoc* (SEVPEN, Paris, 1966).

E. Miller, *The Abbey and Bishopric of Ely* (Cambridge University Press, 1951).

R.H. Hilton, *Social Structures of Rural Warwickshire in the Middle Ages* (Oxford University Press, 1950).

J.A. Raftis, *Tenure and Mobility, Studies in the Social History of the English Villages* (Pontifical Institute of Medieval Studies, Toronto, 1964).

J. Klein, *The Mesta: a Study in Spanish Economic History* (Harvard University Press, 1920).

R. Chazan, *Medieval Jewry in Northern France* (Johns Hopkins University, 1973).

C. Verlinden, *L'esclavage dans l'Europe médiévale*, I (Université de Ghent, Bruges, 1955).

(b) *Particular periods or problems*

A. Havighurst, ed., *The Pirenne Thesis* (Heath, Lexington Mass., 1958).

A.R. Lewis, *The Northern Seas: Shipping and Commerce, A.D. 300–1100* (Princeton University Press, 1958).

P.H. Sawyer, *The Age of the Vikings* (Arnold, London, 1962).

R.L. Reynolds, *Europe Emerges: Transition toward an Industrial Society* (University of Wisconsin Press, Madison, 1961).

J.Z. Titow, *English Rural Society, 1200–1350* (Allen and Unwin, London, 1969).

B. Kedar, *Merchants in Crisis, 1270–1400* (Yale University Press, 1975).

Villages désertés et histoire économique, XI–XVIIIe siècles (SEVPEN, Paris, 1965).

J. Glénisson and J. Day, *Textes et documents d'histoire du moyen âge, XIV–XVe siècles, I: Les "crises" et leur cadre* (SEDES, Paris, 1970).

Les constructions civiles d'intérêt public dans les villes d'Europe au moyen âge (PRO CIVITATE, Brussels, 1971).

G.H.T. Kimble, *Geography in the Middle Ages* (London, 1935).

J.W. Baldwin, *The Medieval Theories of the Just Price* (American Philosophical Society, Philadelphia, 1956).

B. Tierney, *Medieval Poor Law* (University of California Press, Berkeley, 1959).

E. Coornaert, *Les corporations en France avant 1789* (Paris, 1949).

C.M. Cipolla, *Literacy and Development in the West* (Penguin, Harmondsworth, 1969).

W.M. Bowski, *The Finance of the Commune of Siena* (Clarendon, Oxford, 1970).

(c) *Production, demand, labor, and communications*

R. Dion, *Histoire de la vigne et du vin en France* (Doullens, Paris, 1959).

E. Fournial, *Les villes et l'économie d'échange en Forez, XIIIe et XIVe siècles* (Paris, 1967).

D. Knoop and G.P. Jones, *The Mediaeval Mason* (Manchester University Press, 1967).

E. Power, *The Wool Trade in English Medieval History* (Oxford University Press, 1941).

A.R. Bridbury, *England and the Salt Trade in the Later Middle Ages* (Oxford, 1955).

C.M. Cipolla, *Clocks and Culture* (London, 1967).

B. Geremek, *Le salariat dans l'artisanat parisien du XIIIe au XVe siècle* (Paris, 1968).

F.C. Lane, *Navires et constructeurs à Venise pendant la Renaissance*

(SEVPEN, Paris, 1965, a revised translation of an earlier book in English).

C. Gaier, *L'industrie et le commerce des armes dans les anciennes principautés belges* (Les Belles Lettres, Paris, 1973).

J.E. Tyler, *The Alpine Passes, 962–1250* (Blackwell, Oxford, 1930).

Productivity was the theme of the third international conference of Prato, which is to appear shortly.

IV: PERIODICALS, SERIALS, COLLECTED ESSAYS

Some of the most important essays have appeared in collected works by a distinguished scholar, or in his honor. Of these publications, too, only a few examples can be listed here: the studies in honor of Gino Luzzatto, Lucien Febvre, Armando Sapori, Robert L. Reynolds, Fernand Braudel, and the collected studies of Marc Bloch, M.M. Postan, Hans van Werveke are mines of information and ideas. No less important are the published proceedings of international conferences, such as those of the Conférences internationales d'Histoire économique (Stockholm, 1960; Aix-en-Provence, 1962; Munich, 1965, etc.) and those of the Istituto Internazionale di Storia Economica Francesco Datini (Prato, annually since 1968).

Specialized magazines are indispensable to keep up with current research and discussions, both for the articles they contain and for the bibliography they bring up to date. The most important are, in alphabetical order: *Annales (Economies, Sociétés, Civilisations* (formerly entitled *Annales d'Histoire Economique et Sociale*); *Anuario de Historia económica y social; Economia e storia; Economic History Review; Journal of Economic History; Journal of European Economic History; Journal of Social and Economic History of the Orient; Past and Present; Scandinavian Economic History Review; Vierteljahrschrift für Sozial- und Wirtschaftsgeschichte.* But there are significant contributions also in magazines of a more restricted scope, and often in magazines of general history or general economics. Economic historians may soon have to resort to abstracts, as scientists have for a long time; which would be a pity, for no tabulation or summary can entirely represent the detail.

Index